Steel in His Soul

Steel in His Soul

by
Jan Winebrenner

Overseas Crusades

(a division of OC Ministries)

Portions of chapters 3 to 17 contain excerpts from two books written by Dick Hillis. Per his instructions and the approval of Overseas Crusades, the author has rewritten portions of these excerpts, edited them, and placed them all in third person for the purpose of this book:

China Assignment (Palo Alto, Calif.: Overseas Crusades, n.d.), pp. 7-15, 20-23, 27-30, 33-35, 38-44, 47-51, 54-56.
Unlock the Heavens (Henderson, Neb.: Service, n.d.), pp. 10, 15-20, 23-31, 33-40, 42-48, 50-54, 56-61.

All Scripture quotations, unless noted otherwise, are from the King James Version.

Library of Congress Cataloging in Publication Data

Winebrenner, Jan.
  Steel in his soul.

  Bibliography: p.
  1. Hillis, Dick. 2. Missionaries—China—Biography.
3. Missionaries—United States—Biography. I. Title.
BV3427.H543W56 1985 226'.0092'4 [B] 84-27161
ISBN 0-8024-2203-9 (pbk.)

2 3 4 5 6 7 Printing/AF/Year 90 89 88 87 86 85

Printed in the United States of America

Contents

Acknowledgments

My heart goes out in thanksgiving to God for His patience and loving kindness to me. He who began a good work over half a century ago will continue it until He returns to take me home. What grace!

Words from the Apostle Paul light my mind. He writes: "God has chosen the foolish . . . weak . . . base . . . despised . . . things which are not" (1 Corinthians 1:27-28). These words suggest God's kindness to those of us who are His ordinary people.

Although you and I have done nothing to deserve it, God has chosen us. His place of service for me was China. There He allowed me the privilege of working under the godly leadership of the China Inland Mission. Those strong veterans of spiritual warfare taught and encouraged me. There He gave me my loving wife, Margaret, who courageously stood with me no matter how dark, difficult, or dangerous the day. For these things I am thankful.

I want to thank Jan Winebrenner for her labor of love in writing this record. If there are mistakes I take full responsibility—my memory has played me false. I am sorry that names of many friends and fellow-workers who profoundly influenced my walk and work will not be found here. Space did not allow. But each was a messenger of God, sent to help along the Father's path for me. They are in my heart forever.

I pray that our Savior will receive glory and you will be strengthened through the pages of this book.

DICK HILLIS

A word of thanks to my husband, Ken, for his encouragement and support during the hours of work on this project. And to my children, Matthew and Molly, who listened to and critiqued many of the exciting episodes during bedtime devotions, thank you.

To Michael Obel, a special thanks for his meticulous reading of this manuscript. His expertise as a journalist and critic was invaluable.

JAN WINEBRENNER

Preface

Dick Hillis is an adventurer.

His is the story of a man who plunged with abandon into the will of God. It is the story of the ever-widening circles that have revolved around that dive into obedience.

He has been entertained by presidents. He has been ousted by regimes. He has been sought after for his skills and threatened with death because of them.

His is a story that crosses continents and penetrates cultures.

It is also the story of Jesus Christ and His church in the twentieth century.

"To have found God and still to pursue Him is the soul's paradox of love," wrote A. W. Tozer in *The Pursuit of God*. In that sense the story of Dick Hillis is also a love story. His life is a record of his continual seeking after an ever-deepening intimacy with God.

In Dick there is all that is human, vulnerable, and weak. Perhaps that is what makes his story worthwhile. For in contrast with the human spirit the Holy Spirit is able to shine brightly in a man. It is through the powerful presence of the Spirit that the commonplace events of a man's life become inspiring and the common man becomes uncommon.

1

Rebel's Road

The main street of Monroe, Washington, lay silent and dark under late-night shadows. Its narrow, run-down sidewalks were empty now of the merchants and pedestrians who daily filled the path with the noises of business and friendly conversation. Only one figure stood in the darkness, his anxious face peering into the night. His eyes darted first one direction, then another.

Standing in front of the town's drugstore, Dick Hillis took a deep breath to steady himself. Giving one last look down the street, he turned his attention to the store's locked door. His hands shook, rattling the doorknob as he fumbled with the keys. Finally the lock turned, and he was inside the drugstore. With another deep breath he controlled the trembling of his limbs and crossed the few steps to the cash register on the store's counter.

With quiet speed he counted out only as much money as he thought he would need to buy a one-way ticket out of town. He left the rest inside the register drawer to make it appear untouched. He hoped the theft would go undetected, at least for a day or so. He needed time to get as far away as possible.

Escape had been in the seventeen-year-old's mind for a long time. The climax of his dreams was finally within his grasp. With the money tucked in his pockets he let himself out of the store and locked the door behind him.

He grinned. He'd been clever to go to work for the store's owner this summer. And lucky, too—he knew that. It was 1930. His class's high school graduation three months earlier had flooded the tiny town with young job-seekers. Times were hard, and jobs were scarce. He knew he'd been one of the fortunate ones.

The storekeeper had been eager to trust him, glad to have someone in charge when he felt the urge to leave with a bottle of whiskey for a few hours. So in a short time Dick received a key to the store. But it took only a few weeks for Dick to be convinced that the life of a shopkeeper was not the life for him.

The farmboy had dreams too big for a small town like Monroe. He had dreams of wealth and adventure, travel and excitement. And he determined nothing would stop him from realizing those dreams.

No one would suspect that he was the thief. He told his parents that morning that he was going to visit an aunt living in Seattle, so there would be no mystery surrounding his sudden disappearance.

Dick made his way to the bus depot where he bought a ticket to Seattle. Then he carefully counted his change. There wasn't much, but he was sure he would survive until he could find work. His goal was the docks that hugged the port city.

For years he had fantasized about joining the crew of a vessel bound for China. His imagination had conjured up visions of mystery and intrigue surrounding that land. He knew he would never be content until he sailed into Shanghai.

He spent one night with his aunt in Seattle, just long enough to lend truth to the story he told his parents. But the next morning he left quickly and headed for the shipyards.

Dick could hardly control the tremors of anticipation that swept over him as he walked slowly through the dock area, turning first one way then another, trying to take in all the sights around him. His eyes glittered with excitement as he gazed at the huge ships, their gangplanks crowded with men carrying crates aboard, the hurrying sailors, the massive cranes lifting burdens onto already heaving decks.

This was it—the beginning of the realization of his dreams. The view in front of him blurred into visions of silken treasures and mysterious cities. He shook himself and looked around again, pulling himself back to reality. *First things first,* he told himself. He marched toward the office building that bore the sign "Merchant Marines."

Clutching a bag of meager belongings, the teenager, sturdily built but not tall, stood in front of the Merchant Marine officer. It took every ounce of his willpower to contain his excitement in the presence of this man who had the ability to grant him his greatest wish.

"Sorry, son. You're only seventeen. That's too young. We can't take you on."

The words slapped Dick in the face.

Too young? Oh, why hadn't he lied about his age? He would have if he had known. He lied about most other things. Why did he have to tell the truth this time?

The damage was done, and there was no undoing it. He would just have to try farther down the coast. Squaring his shoulders, he turned and walked out of the office. A short time later he was on the side of the highway, hitchhiking south to San Francisco. There must be a ship there bound for China. Surely someone would be glad to hire an eager, strong youth who wasn't afraid of hard work.

But it was the same story in San Francisco.

"Sorry, boy. You're not old enough."

No matter what he said, Dick couldn't persuade anyone to hire him as a ship's crewman. The glamor of his adventure began to fade in the glare of harsh reality: he was a long way from home now and tired, and he had very little money left.

The long hours of the third night found him huddling in the dark and dangerous shadows of the San Francisco dock, sleeping little and wondering what his next move would be.

He had two choices: he could go on or go home. When he thought about it, he knew he couldn't go home. What if the store owner had discovered the theft? What if the police suspected him? He would have to go on. There was still more California coastline, and there had to be more ships bound for China.

In the darkness of the San Francisco docks, the reality of his situation penetrated his mind. He knew there was nothing to gain by going south. It would be the same story: "Sorry kid, you're too young."

The next morning Dick stretched his stiff, cold muscles and headed reluctantly toward the highway to begin his trek back up the coast toward Seattle. During the miserable night hours he had made up his mind to confess to his crime. He would ask his parents' forgiveness and ask the storekeeper if he could work for him until the debt was repaid.

Then, he thought, *I'll really leave Monroe. But it will be with a clear conscience, and I'll never come back again!*

As he stood alone and lonely on the side of the highway, his thumb stabbing the cold morning air, his thoughts turned to his twin brother, Don. Don had left Monroe about the same time Dick ran away. He had gone south too, but not for shipyards and adventure. His destination had been the Bible Institute of Los Angeles.

Don always knew what his next move was. He seemed to know what he wanted out of life. That perplexed Dick. How could a man want to be a minister? Yet that seemed to be what Don wanted. The boys' grandfather had been a strong spiritual influence on Don. And it was at his prompting that Don had decided to go to a Bible school to study for the ministry.

It was hard for Dick to visualize his identical twin in a clerical role, though Don always had been the more serious of the two. The twins had spent most of their lives in mischief, with Dick as instigator. Their high school had been relieved when the boys, most particularly Dick, finally graduated.

Monroe High School's biology class had been the scene of more than a few misdemeanors. One fiasco in the lab was never to be forgotten. Dick grinned at the memory.

"Hey, Bud, sing!" Dick had one day commanded his football buddy, who sat on a nearby stool in the lab.

Bud opened his mouth to sing, and Dick flipped the end of his dissecting knife to catapult the guts of his laboratory frog right into his friend's mouth. Not to be outdone, Bud emptied the black contents of his fountain pen across the front of Dick's white shirt. Chaos followed.

The young teacher, only a year out of college, struggled to regain control of the classroom. In a frenzy she fought to disentangle her high heels from the rungs of the lab stool. As the stool began to tip she shrieked, grabbing vainly for something to hold on to. The high stool crashed over backward, taking the teacher with it, her feet still caught in the rungs. The two gallant troublemakers rushed to pick her up before they took refuge in the boys' washroom for the rest of the day.

Dick and Don both shared credit for the plan to throw rotten eggs into the school's air circulation system. The huge fans blew the stench through every hall and classroom in the building.

But the climax of Dick's academic life came on graduation night. The administration, which had agreed to rent the seniors' graduation caps and gowns, decided not to pay after all. On graduation day the students were told they would have to pay for their own. In a small farming town during the Depression that was a serious financial matter.

"If you're not going to pay for them, like you agreed," shouted a defiant Dick to the principal, "then nobody is going to wear one. It's not fair for only the kids who can afford them to have them. The whole class is graduating, not just the rich kids!"

And so the escapade was on: hide the caps and gowns from the administration. A few students managed to get hold of theirs before the rest were tucked out of sight. The faculty issued its ultimatum: no caps and gowns, no graduation.

Dick was not intimidated.

"We already have our grades. You can't fail us! And you're not getting those caps and gowns, either!"

A riot broke out in the auditorium when only the names of the "clad grads" were called up to receive their diplomas.

This was front page news in the tiny, quiet town of Monroe, Washington, that June of 1930. And it made the headlines of the following day's paper, *The Monroe Monitor:*

STUDENTS START RIOT ON GRADUATION NIGHT

In the smaller print Dick was named as instigator.

Three months later, Monroe was not sorry to say good-bye to the young man whose restlessness and rebellion had made his name synonymous with disturbance and disaster.

What kind of welcome would the town hold for him now—a thief and a runaway returned home with his tail between his legs? He had many miles of Pacific coastline to contemplate the reaction of his parents and the store owner. As each mile passed he grew more anxious and fearful.

But his fears were needless. His parents welcomed him home with tears and forgiveness. He knew things might be quite different when he confessed to the store owner, but his parents' support gave him courage.

"I'm willing to go to the authorities and confess what I've done, if you want me to. But I'd like the chance to work for you until I've repaid what I stole from you," said a nervous Dick. He held his breath while he waited for the man's reply. If he insisted on criminal charges, Dick could face a sentence in the juvenile reformatory near Monroe. But the old man was content to let Dick work off the debt, and once again, Dick found himself behind the counter of the drugstore.

The days were long and miserable for the energetic youth whose hunger for excitement and adventure had not been satisfied by his journey down the coastal highway to San Francisco. He grew more restless with each passing day. He missed his brother and lately had been growing curious about the school in Los Angeles where Don was studying.

"Mom, Dad, it's been three weeks now, and I've just about worked off my debt. What would you think if I went to school in Los Angeles with Don? I don't have any other prospects right now, and I think I'd like to try it."

Harry and Frances tried to hide their excitement. For years they had prayed for this boy, their rebel son. Saying little about the fact that it was a Bible school, they encouraged him to apply, even though it was already a few weeks into the first semester.

Dick packed his few clothes and, with the help of $15 from his older brother, Harry, Jr., he bought a bus ticket to Los Angeles.

Dick arrived in Los Angeles and, after a night on campus in Don's room, he made an appointment with the dean of the Bible institute.

"I'd like to enroll," Dick stated to the dean. "I know the semester started weeks ago, but I'd like to stay."

"I think we would be able to accept you as a student," replied the dean, "but you'll have to fill out these admission papers."

Dick sat down with a pencil and began filling out the form. One question related to funds. How much did he have available? Dick fumbled in his pocket and counted his change: $1.20. He wrote the amount on the form and wondered, *Will that keep me out?* But he did not really believe it would, because he was sure Don hadn't much more than that.

The next question on the form confused him. "When were you saved?" Dick had no idea what that meant, but he wrote, "When I was born."

Dick handed the completed form to the dean and waited for his decision. The dean read through the information. When he came to Dick's answer about when he was saved, he paused and looked up at the boy. Something inside him reached out to the young man who had come so far on so little. In every line of the boy's taut frame he could read an eagerness for discovery, the anticipation of dreams fulfilled. In this place it was possible he would make his greatest discovery—that of God's infinite, limitless love for him.

Without another thought, the dean wrote across the application, "Accepted on three months' probation."

Dick thanked the dean and left the office. When he reached Don's room he let his excitement burst forth. "Don, I'm in, I'm in!" he shouted. "I made it!"

It was a different sort of adventure from what the Washington farmboy had anticipated. But, he had to admit, being in school in southern California excited him. He knew he faced hours of studies and lectures and much hard work. What he did not know was that he had embarked on an adventure that would alter his life forever. He had no idea he had in fact stepped onto the path that would ultimately bring him to China.

2

Journey into Faith

Charles Richard (Dick) and Donald Whitman Hillis, identical twin boys, rushed into life on February 13, 1913, in Victoria, British Columbia. Impulsive, presumptuous behavior was an early precedent—they were two months premature.

The doctors warned their parents that it was possible that neither of the tiny infants would survive. Their father, a man of action, immediately hired a live-in nurse to help take care of them. It was thirteen months before the boys were out of danger and the nurse could be released.

Harry, Jr., the twins' older brother, was a quiet, handsome boy, much like his mother. He was good at everything he tried, yet too often people made over the twins and neglected their older brother.

As they grew, the children spent many hours on their uncle's nearby farm. It was there that Dick made his first acquaintance with Chinese people.

Using all the creative genius he possessed, Dick teased and tormented the Chinese laborers employed on his uncle's farm. His pranks were as merciless as they were imaginative. Eventually the workers retaliated by chasing their tormentor and pulling his hair, yelling in their sing-song voices and calling down curses on the troublesome boy.

Out of immature prejudice, Dick grouped all Chinese into one category: mean and cantankerous. His only experience had taught him to fear and dislike them all.

While Dick was still in grade school, the family moved to Monroe,

Washington, to take up life on a dairy farm. It was a small, poor farm, needing the help of every member of the family to keep it running. The boys spent evenings milking cows, mucking stalls, and tending to whatever chores suited their sizes and abilities.

The family's social life revolved around the little Methodist church in town. Whenever the doors of the church were open, the Hillis family was present.

In 1926, the pastor of the church scheduled a week of evangelistic meetings. It was a special event for the entire farming community. The guest speaker was Dr. George Bennard, author of the already famous and well-loved hymn "The Old Rugged Cross."

Dick was thirteen, and the prospect of going to church every night for a week did not hold any special allure for him. Yet he could see some advantages—a welcome escape from homework and a chance to be with the gang. So he stifled his protests and went each evening with only minimal argument.

The week of meetings passed slowly, each evening much like the night before: sing a hymn, take the offering, preach, sing again, offer invitation, sing another stanza, pray, and—at last—go home.

But Thursday was different. Something happened to Dick that night.

The content of Dr. Bennard's message was much like all his other sermons, and Dick had heard it all before. In fact, much earlier in the week he had stopped listening altogether. But when the service drew to a close, and the invitation to accept Jesus Christ as Savior was offered, Dick felt deep stirrings of conviction inside himself, a compelling sense of being called to go to China as a missionary.

No one was more surprised than Dick himself when he suddenly pushed his way out of the pew and rushed to the front altar of the church.

I'll go, his heart answered.

Excitement, exuberance, and longing filled the young boy at his first experience of commitment. But confusion tickled his mind, too. He had no idea of what being a missionary meant. He had only an intense compulsion, a sense of being drawn to that Oriental country, and a vague idea of "serving God."

This was a strange admission from the boy raised by Harry and Frances Hillis, for they were godly, loving parents who were devoted to Jesus Christ.

Frances had a rich spiritual heritage dating back to the Zwingli crusades of an earlier century. She had been raised by godly parents and learned as a child to love and study the Bible. Her musical talents took her to study at Oberlin Conservatory of Music in an era when few women pursued college degrees.

Dick's father, Harry, was a self-taught Bible student. Though he had completed only three years of high school, he was a respected teacher of men's Bible studies.

Dick observed his parents' Christianity—their worship, prayer, and Bible study. And he participated in the church activities. But he didn't understand the principles of faith that were at work in his parents' lives.

Their faith was a private thing. Both Harry and Frances were quiet, reserved individuals. The expression of their deepest thoughts and emotions was not easy for them. Though their faith was active, they did not articulate it to Dick in a way that he could understand. They were rich in spiritual knowledge, but they seemed unable to share it with Dick.

In the more pragmatic affairs of the church they were better able to communicate within their family. And so missionary involvement was well understood by all the Hillises. The boys put their extra pennies in a bowl each week. When enough was collected the amount was sent to missionaries. Daily prayer for missionaries was an activity in which everyone in the house participated.

When Dick was very small he heard the story of Aunt Plythe, his father's aunt, who had gone to India as a missionary. The account of her death in a famine in that country made a profound impression on his young mind.

So, while church and faith had little personal meaning for him as he was growing up, his first stirrings of spiritual response took the form of a missionary calling. But there can be no doubt that the undefined longing to "serve God" that he felt at the altar originated in those early years. The calling to the mission field had long been upheld in his family as a noble summons.

But that undefined longing dissipated not long after its first tuggings were felt. His desire to be a missionary floundered in high school. Soon Dick's only longings were for fun and football. His grades were good, but he often resorted to cheating if that seemed necessary.

The dream of China never died, but the purpose for going was displaced by another. In his sophomore year of high school he read a novel about a jewel thief who went to Shanghai and found his fortune. A new desire began to swell in Dick.

Instead of going to China as a missionary to bring something to its people, he began to see China as the place where he could claim riches for himself. It represented fame and excitement. In his dreams he went to China and returned as a conquering hero—rich and powerful.

The dream of China also represented escape. He loved his parents, yet disliked the poverty of their life. He cared about them, yet he cared little for their faith. Money and excitement were his cravings.

And in his pursuit for those things, he was blind to the pain he was inflicting on his parents.

Dick often went out at night with his friends, and only the firm discipline of his father brought him home before dawn the next day. But one night his father was away on business, and Dick stayed out until the early morning hours. As he crept in, passing his mother's room, he was sure he had escaped her discovery. But as he paused outside her door he heard crying. He peeked through the crack of the doorway and saw her on her knees beside her bed.

"Send me to hell if need be," she sobbed, "but don't let my Dick go!"

Fear gripped him like a vise. His rebellion was under seige.

I have to get away, he thought in panic. If he didn't, he might succumb to their prayers. He might have to give up his dreams.

The day after hearing the prayers of his weeping mother he started planning his escape. He would rob the drugstore and buy a ticket to Seattle and the docks. There he would board a ship and sail to China and his destiny.

But things didn't go as he planned. Instead of signing on as a crew member of a ship bound for China, he signed up as a student at Biola—the Bible Institute of Los Angeles.

Dick's first month in school proved miserable. The Washington farmboy was no stranger to the hard work necessary to pay for his tuition expenses. That he faced with confidence and the strength of youth. But he was as a foreigner in the classes when the Bible was being discussed. Christian jargon was jibberish to him. He had no idea of doctrine or terminology. His excitement began to wane.

Then, in the third month, everything changed.

It was November 14, a Sunday night. Dick and Don attended a preaching service at the Church of the Open Door. That night, for the first time, the truth of Jesus Christ became clear to Dick. He saw the Savior; he saw himself as a sinner. And he made Jesus Christ his Lord.

The rebellion ended, and the restlessness was put to rest. Dick found and embraced the One his parents quietly served. He was new inside, and he knew it.

Unknown to Dick, that same night his brother, Don, experienced for himself the love and salvation of Jesus Christ. For he, too, had had only secondhand knowledge of Christ.

Now studies took on new meaning. The Bible became not only a textbook for the classroom but the guidebook for living. Don renewed his commitment to the ministry but with an understanding of its meaning. And Dick determined to discover God's plan for his life. He became absorbed in his studies. He found the Bible fascinating. His grades were good, and his knowledge of God grew along with his understanding of His Word.

When he attended his first missionary conference during that semester he again experienced the pull to become a missionary. Again China's allure tugged at something deep inside him. And again, his soul answered with a resounding yes.

But Dick was troubled and uncertain. Was it really God's voice calling him to China? Or was it just the intrigue of the Oriental land that had captured his imagination in childhood and still held it?

There was time to settle the issue of which direction God wanted him to go. Meanwhile, there were other, more pressing matters to concern himself with, for example, where was his next meal going to come from? How was he going to pay for his books and lodging this semester?

His newfound faith grew as it was daily tested and stretched. Those were difficult days for most Americans, with the Great Depression just months from its apex. Dick, along with other students, was eager for any odd job that was available. He mowed lawns, ran errands, did anything that would provide money for room, board, shoes, books. He had to trust God to provide for every need from toothpaste to tuition.

Eventually that simple, day-by-day trust would mature to the point that he could stare boldly down the barrel of a Communist soldier's rifle. But he began his journey into courage and obedience by learning to trust God to supply his simplest needs.

3

Road to China

Sovereignty or irony? There can be no question of the guiding hand of God moving in the experiences of a Washington farmboy brought face to face with the Person who would change his life. Gone was the cocky, defiant rebel. In his place was a new Dick, one who now felt compelled to share the reality of Jesus Christ in his life.

He took advantage of every opportunity to tell others about what had happened in his heart and what Christ could do for anyone who would accept Him. He taught Sunday school classes, preached in street meetings, shared the love of Jesus with inmates at local jails, and went into the slums of Los Angeles to testify in rescue missions.

In the flurry of activities the school year passed quickly. Dick and Don were soon on their way home to spend the summer of 1931 with their family in Monroe.

That summer Dick accepted his most ambitious preaching assignment. The pastor of the Methodist church where Dick had grown up asked him to speak during a Sunday night service. Word of the "new" Dick spread quickly through the small town. Everyone knew the prodigal had returned. And the church was filled to capacity.

Dick stood up as the pastor introduced him that Sunday night. Looking out over the congregation he saw many of his high school friends staring back at him curiously. *Will they listen,* he wondered, as he cleared his throat nervously. *Or will they be skeptical and cynical?*

With a quick prayer, he opened his Bible and began to speak.

It was a gentler, humbler Dick who told of the love and mercy of God in sending His Son, Jesus, so that one like him could have a new life. What had happened to the troublemaker, the rebellious upstart who wasn't afraid of anybody? He was gone, and in his place stood someone who spoke of submission, repentance, forgiveness, and a loving Savior. After he finished, Don gave a clear testimony of how he too had met the Savior.

Their friends couldn't help but listen to the young men who spoke with such conviction and excitement about the love of Jesus. That night two of their friends followed them into faith in Christ.

The summer passed quickly. Dick was excited about getting back to his studies. He was determined to find out just exactly what God's plan for him included—China, or something else. He grew anxious to know for certain whether China was his fantasy or God's calling.

"I've no doubt You want me in Your service as a missionary, Lord," he prayed. "But I've got to be *sure* that it's really China where You want me. I don't want to tell You where I want to go. I want *You* to tell *me* where You want me to go."

Dick was convinced that God would make His will clear to him. And with that conviction he plunged himself into the pool of school activities. He studied, preached, taught classes, and concentrated on learning all he could about Jesus Christ in his daily life. As the weeks passed he began to feel satisfied with his ministry and his life.

He became so satisfied with his life and work and all the opportunities for service that thoughts of going to a foreign land—*any* foreign land—to serve God became fewer. There was so much to be done right here, he reasoned. Why should he go somewhere else?

The dream of China was fading.

Dick knew that part of the reason for that was the sight of a lovely girl. He first saw her at a Biola banquet, and from that night he could not get Margaret Humphrey off his mind. He watched her in class. He used any excuse to get close enough to talk with her. His first date with her—a tennis game—was also his last. She began going steady with one of his best friends.

But Dick refused to give up hope. He wrote her name on the top of his prayer list and asked God to give her to him. She became his one concern, more important than the destiny of China or the needs of a man across the street.

Then God used a class on Romans to force Dick to see again the desperate condition of men on either side of the ocean. As the class moved through the first three chapters of Romans, the Holy Spirit taught him and illuminated the truth of man's fate without Jesus Christ. The awfulness of millions being lost set up a conflict in young Dick's mind. For a time he questioned, _Is God really love?_

But as he struggled and studied, the Holy Spirit took him to the hill of Calvary. He realized that the love and holiness, the wrath and justice of God are all part of His perfect character. He saw God's righteous wrath toward sin and His abiding love toward the sinner.

As he meditated on the words "He that spared not his own Son" (Romans 8:32), Dick was satisfied that God loves lost mankind. At that point he heard the cry of the millions across the sea. They became his personal responsibility. He could not, nor did he want to, avoid the searching questions asked in the book of Romans:

"How then shall they call on Him [to save them] in whom they have not believed? and how shall they believe in Him of whom they have not heard? and how shall they hear without a preacher? And how shall they preach, except they be sent?" (Romans 10:14-15).

But the question of China still plagued him. Was his desire to go there simply part of his boyhood dream? He set about to find out. Each week he went to the library to study the people and customs of a different country. He bought a _National Geographic_ world map, and in alphabetical order he prayed for different countries each day. He made it a point to hear every missionary speaker possible. He read every missionary biography he could get his hands on.

Dick sought out missionaries to question them about their work and the needs on their fields. In order to understand "faith missions" he asked three to put him on their mailing lists.

The more he searched the more intense grew the conviction that God did want him to serve in China. And there seemed to be as many obstacles to being a servant in China as there were to being an adventurer there. The language loomed as the largest obstacle.

God knew, better than he, that language was by far his poorest subject. Even with a sympathetic teacher and some special tutoring, the best grade he had made in Spanish was a _D_. It was illogical that he should go to China—to a people whose language is one of the most difficult in the world.

Another obstacle was the tonal quality of the Chinese language. Dick considered himself to be only one grade point above tone deaf. To his way of thinking, one should be musical to speak the language and artistic to write its characters. And he was neither musical nor artistic.

Could he, in the face of such shortcomings, really expect to retain thousands of Chinese characters—characters that to his untrained eyes looked like they were written by a drunken chicken?

_No,_ he said to himself a hundred times, _it just isn't logical. God does not_ *want me in China. What if I went, flunked the language, and came home a missionary casualty? Such action certainly would not bring glory to God.*

As he struggled with this problem, he was reading through the book of Exodus. Assuring God and attempting to reassure himself that if it were not for the language problem he would gladly go, he opened his Bible to read. That Wednesday morning his reading was in the fourth chapter. In verse ten he was struck with the excuses Moses made for not obeying Jehovah's orders:

"I am not eloquent. . . . I am slow of speech, and of a slow tongue."

Dick's excuses were not too different from the ones Moses made in his encounter with God. But the next verse rebuked the new believer. "And the Lord said unto him, Who hath made man's mouth? . . . have not I the Lord?" In the same way that God had answered Moses' arguments some three thousand years earlier, He now spoke to Dick.

Thoughts raced through his mind with such rapidity they tumbled over one another. In obedience, situations that seem illogical become reasonable. *Will He not enable me to do whatever He appoints me to do?* Dick thought. *Is it not like God to give his servant a task and even send him to the place that is hardest for him so that God's grace can be more fully manifested?*

"Father, I see You have a right to send me any place and that I have a right to expect You to see me through." God's promise to Moses in Exodus 4:12 was enough for Dick: "Now therefore go, and I will be with thy mouth, and teach thee what thou shalt say."

Dick knew that the pull he felt toward China was the summons of God. The issue of whether he should go or stay was settled. But the dilemma he felt at the sight of Margaret Humphrey and the thought of her gentle smile and hazel eyes was still unresolved.

4

Vanishing Halo

Dick had no idea what he was getting into.

At twenty he was the youngest American missionary candidate ever accepted by the China Inland Mission—and probably its most naive as well. It was 1933. China was a land in constant turmoil. The communist ideology was advancing insidiously into the ancient civilization, and internal warring erupted without warning. Danger, as well as difficulty, lay ahead.

But young Dick felt only optimism. He was full of exuberance and enthusiasm. He stood on the threshold of fulfilling his greatest dream. With the diploma from the Bible institute in his hand and his financial support secured he packed his bags and waited only to say the final good-byes.

Though it was the twentieth century, the China that awaited him had changed little from the China of 1850 of which Hudson Taylor had said, "Poor neglected China! Scarcely anyone cares about it. And that immense country, containing nearly a fourth of the human race, is left in ignorance and darkness."

From its seaports to its rugged mountain terrains, from its fields and farming villages to its rivers and inland walled cities, it had still heard little of the life-changing truth of the one true God and His Son, Jesus.

But Dick cared about China with all his heart. His boyhood dream of a Marco Polo's Orient had given way to a new vision. Now, instead of seeing a land rich with mystery and silken treasures, he saw the misery of men and women dying without Christ, living without hope.

Nothing would deter him from the purpose he now held in his heart: to bring them Jesus and His new life. But nothing could prepare him for the China he would find.

Others, veterans of the work in that vast country, knew that the task of the missionary there was difficult at best, and sometimes seemed impossible. China's long-standing resentment of outside influence made her culture difficult to penetrate with new beliefs. Her internal political conditions further complicated the missionary's task.

But in the face of those handicaps, Dick was confident and convinced he was God's man for China. He focused only on heaven's gain and denied all possibility of the pain that might accompany it. In addition to his youthful idealism he possessed a sense of self-righteousness. He was certain he would not fail. He, the youngest and surely the most earnest of the mission's appointees, *could* not fail.

It wasn't entirely his fault that he seemed to be wearing a halo. Others seemed to see it too.

"Isn't he wonderful to give up such a promising career at home to go to China?" the ladies would exclaim each time he spoke at a women's missionary meeting.

Sometimes he heard, "Oh, I can't remember when I have seen such a committed man, so young, and making so many sacrifices for the gospel's sake."

By the time he was ready to board the *Empress of Canada* bound for China, he had no doubt he would accomplish in China what no one had yet been able to do. His halo and his head had been expanded by shaft after shaft of lighted glory. But Dick soon learned that as the fiery heat of the sun burns away the halo around the moon, so the fiery trials of foreign service melt the halo around a missionary's head.

Shortly after he lost sight of his native land he became disturbed by a sense of loneliness. This was no eight-day excursion. This trip was the beginning of an eight-year separation from his family and his friends. Dick was more alone than he had ever been before.

During the voyage, traveling third class on a rolling ship plowing slowly toward China, his loneliness increased. Most of the other third-class passengers were Chinese, so conversation was impossible. He grew sorry for himself, and the halo began to fade.

But he did not give up with the first heat of battle. He fought back! "Loneliness might defeat a soldier with less stamina, but not me!" he exclaimed. And he meditated on the promise Jesus gave in Matthew 28:18, 20: "All power is given unto me . . . . and lo, I am with you alway." He claimed that promise, chalked up a victory, and readjusted his halo.

The long voyage passed slowly, but finally they reached Shanghai. Dick stood on the deck of the ship and watched as they pulled into the harbor. The thrill of seeing China for the first time filled his chest with a mingling of pain and joy he had never felt before. China! His new homeland!

Sights and sounds assaulted his senses—the sing-song Oriental voices raised in anger and laughter, barking out brisk commands; the strange-looking conveyances called rickshas rolling along narrow, winding streets. He wanted to see it all, feel and hear all of China in that one first moment.

The gangplank was lowered, and Dick made his way down to the dock area. Somehow he was able to communicate with a coolie, who helped him carry his suitcases.

As he walked along the narrow cobblestone street, absorbing every new and fascinating sight, the first sensations of fear crept into his spirit. He was an alien in a foreign land.

Suddenly another of his senses was attacked—the sense of smell! The stench of human dung permeated the air. He learned later that collectors carried "honey buckets" from house to house each day to pick up refuse. Then it was taken to the fields and buried to be brought up later for fertilizer. But at that moment, with the malodor heavy in the air, he was filled with anxiety and revulsion. _How can I stay here?_ he wondered.

But just then the path led past a tiny graveyard. Small mud mounds were marked by stones, and bits of weeds and grass grew here and there.

He was jarred back into remembering why he had come. And he asked himself then, _How can I leave?_ He was certain that most of the mounds represented souls that had died without Christ.

Dick's first days in China were filled with official appointments, meetings, and constant activity. He was too busy to be homesick. After two weeks in Shanghai it was time to repack for a trip upriver to the language school, where he would begin the difficult task of studying Chinese.

It was a slow journey up the Yangtze River by riverboat, but the sights and glimpses into China's river people made it fascinating. Dick was too enthralled with the novelties around him to even think of loneliness. Could anyone be lonely with all the promise of adventure and discovery in this turbulent land?

The boat arrived at the town of Anking in the early morning hours of the third day. While the captain held the boat steady in midstream, the passengers jumped into a flimsy _san-pan_ and two sleepy coolies poled them to the north bank of the river through waters too shallow for the riverboat.

At language school in the old city of Anking, Dick found that here too there was no time for loneliness. The days were busy from five in the morning until eleven at night with classes on mission orientation, Chinese culture, and the new language. And each class demanded hours of homework.

Night after night Dick sat at his desk reading, memorizing, and copying characters until, exhausted, he collapsed onto the cot in his tiny room. But he wasn't alone in his determination to conquer the difficult sounds and shapes of the strange Chinese characters. Forty other missionaries from a dozen countries shared the same intensity, the same desire to become conversant in Mandarin in order to go out and preach and teach. Though they were cross-cultural, they shared a common goal.

At last the six months of language school were over and Dick was assigned to the densely populated agricultural province of Honan. After days of travel by boat, train, and bike, he reached the inland city of Shenkiu, his first mission station.

The senior missionary in Shenkiu was a Mr. Tomkinson. He and his wife welcomed the young novice. Experienced and energetic, Mr. Tomkinson set a rugged schedule for his trainee: six days of language study followed by three days of witness in some nearby Buddhist village. Before the six days were over Dick wanted to scream that he could not look at another Chinese character, but before the sun set in the village on the third day of preaching, he was eager to get back to the books.

I must *get the language; I must tell the story,* he daily urged himself. *This is war,* he thought. But he was slowly winning, and in the excitement of the battle loneliness dissipated.

Then came a telegram signed by the mission directors: "Request the Tomkinsons move to Hwailien." Just four days later Dick walked out through the city gate with the Tomkinsons and waved good-bye as they rode toward their new assignment.

The walk that led back across the moat, through the great iron gate, and down the main street to the mission house seemed longer than usual. When the cook rang the supper bell Dick did not feel hungry. He forced himself to eat the Chinese noodles, all the while thinking of the things he should have asked Mr. Tomkinson. At one point during the lonely meal he started to speak, but the sight of Mr. Tomkinson's vacant chair stopped him.

That night the house felt empty. By ten o'clock tiredness dimmed his eyes, so he closed the language primer and carried the kerosene lantern upstairs. As he walked through the Tomkinsons' bedroom he recalled that the local Chinese believed the old house to be haunted by evil spirits. Right then it did seem haunted and hollow, and Dick felt very much alone.

"This is nonsense!" he told himself. "God is with me, and tomorrow and everyday afterwards I will be surrounded by Chinese friends." And he climbed into bed and slept.

Busy day followed busy day. At first, only the nights were lonely, but as his skill with the Chinese language increased, so did his desire to hear an English word. He tried talking to himself in English, but that only made him feel foolish. He tried singing but found his own voice difficult to listen to. Reading his Bible aloud in English helped for a time, but that too soon lost its comfort. Dick began to dream of home.

Gradually his spirit seemed to wither and dry up. Praying became a whirl of thought that swept through his mind but never left his lips. He read the Bible as one would read a popular magazine. He preached with no inspiration. Confusion and guilt played havoc with his emotions. It was not long before he was ready to declare his failure and concede defeat. It was in this hour of contemplated retreat that a telegram arrived: "Ten-day conference for defeated missionaries being held in Shansi."

It would mean a three-day bike ride followed by two days by train to get to the conference. It would mean the admission of his desperation and loneliness—

He went.

He felt a flush of embarrassment as he entered the first gathering. His being there signified that he was a defeated man. But there was comfort in realizing all were there for the same reason.

God, Dick prayed silently as he took his seat in group, *You must meet us or we will retreat as casualties from the field of battle.*

Together the missionaries read the Bible. They prayed. Sometimes they wept together. One woman got up from her knees and slipped the engagement ring from her finger. Her engagement was not God's will, she said. She had said yes only because she was lonely. A brokenhearted man sobbed out that he did not love China or her people.

A gray-haired man who was coming to the close of his missionary service asked everyone to get up from their knees. Sitting in a circle they listened to his story of barren years—years that were wasted, he said, because he had tried to do God's work in his own strength. Dick clenched his hands together in his lap. *It's as though he's talking about me,* he thought miserably.

When the group session ended he hurried to his room and locked the door. Kneeling by his bed he saw the halo he had so proudly worn during the past months. It loomed big and brilliant and horrid in his mind's aye. He saw himself, the young hero from California, the darling of the women's missionary societies, so committed to the Lord that he was going to win China for Christ.

He had worked hard. But with sudden clarity he saw that it had been *his* work, not God's. And as the work was his own, so was the defeat. The shame of it all melted his heart. His ears were now ready to hear God speak the words of John 15:5. "For without me," Jesus said, "ye can do nothing."

Never before had Dick really believed that. He, who wore the halo of a missionary—certainly could do something! No, for the first time he knew he could do nothing.

His mind turned to other scriptures that continued to teach him to walk in the Spirit.

"This is it!" Dick said. "The Holy Spirit is to guide. I am to follow and obey."

There was no argument in his heart as he submitted to the Lord. He responded and turned himself over to the Holy Spirit.

"Let Christ be my Lord, and I His servant," he prayed that night.

The heavy cloak of depression lifted. The loneliness subsided. He discovered that missionaries are human. He discovered that God's grace and glory are the only adequate resources for missionaries, for people like him. With that discovery, the halo vanished, and in its place was set a soldier's helmet.

5

Unlocked Heavens

"Come and watch the foreign devils die!"

Coarse, raucous voices called to the villagers and farmers clustered, terrified, in the small town of Tsingteh, in Anhuei province of China. The communist soldiers were rough with hate and fury. They forced the pale-skinned "foreign devils" through the gathering crowd of onlookers. They watched them fall to their knees, exhausted and weak after twenty-four hours of abuse and torture.

Just two days earlier, on December 6, 1934, in the dark morning hours before the sunrise could strike the walls of the village, a small band of rebels stormed through them. The ancient town once known as the "city of kings" fell to the bandits, who may have been communist soldiers. Before they could flee for their lives, John and Betty Stam, missionaries with the China Inland Mission, were captured.

It had been an odd scene in the Stam's tiny home that morning, with Betty serving tea and cakes to the soldiers and then watching as they bound her husband and took him to the army headquarters. Not much later they returned for her.

"We have been abducted," John wrote to the mission headquarters in Shanghai. "They demand twenty thousand dollars for our release . . . we praise God for peace in our hearts and a meal tonight . . . The Lord bless and guide you, and as for us, may God be glorified whether by life or by death."

God's glory was the death of John and Betty Stam. In the early morning of

December 8, 1934, they were stripped of their outer garments, bound by ropes, and marched through the village. The rhythm of death cries from the rebel soldiers beat harsh accompaniment to their march.

On a little hill outside the town John was forced to kneel. Then with a swift flash of the sword his life was ended. Betty fell on her knees beside him as he died. And then once again a shouted command brought the executioner's sword streaking through the air, and Betty too, was struck down.

In an instant Betty and John left the "city of kings" and were ushered into the palace of the King of kings. But the shock of their violent death set off a quake of fear and uncertainty that reverberated throughout the most distant Christian communities of the world. Other CIM missionaries in neighboring provinces received the news of their co-workers' deaths with a mixture of disbelief and terror.

On a cold December morning just days after the Stams' murder, Dick Hillis sat huddled alone in his tiny mud-walled hut in the nearby Honan province. Despair and misery hunched his shoulders as he sat in the dimly lit room trying to keep warm, forcing his mind to fight the waves of sadness that threatened to drown him.

He was twenty-one now. Word of the Stams' execution reached him just as he was completing his first year as a missionary.

At first he felt only numbness. Then, as the reality of the tragedy forced itself upon him, pain pierced his spirit. Great sobs racked him and he cried out with anguish, all the loneliness and frustration of the last few months finally finding release.

"Am I throwing my life away? Will I too, be captured and murdered? Am I going to die here, too, Lord, alone and thousands of miles from home? And for what?" he cried.

The righteous answers that had once been so easy to utter were now difficult to pronounce. His stiff commitment to China's unevangelized millions began to waver.

He had experienced a sense of joyful purpose in the early days after the conference for discouraged missionaries. But all that seemed far away now—beyond his reach. Unspoken questions had begun to gather like storm clouds in recent weeks. Doubts that had lurked in his mind surfaced now with a force that shook him. The spiritual renewal he had known in earlier days seemed dead and buried with the mutilated bodies of his fellow laborers.

"What am I doing here? What good is my life?" he asked.

Agony and despair seemed to have joined hands to form a barrier between him and the peace he once knew. It was too much for the unseasoned soldier. The young recruit who had just spent his first year on the front lines of duty was experiencing battle fatigue that threatened to destroy him.

The insidious whisper of Satan hissed lies into his ear. "Go home. You're wasting your life and you know it. Go back to America. There is nothing here for you."

Dick had once felt he was prepared to fight and die, if need be, for the work of Jesus Christ in China. He had had grand visions of courage in the face of obstacles, but he had never visualized this—the murder of fellow missionaries.

Suddenly alone with grief and fear, he realized he was ready to give up. He saw for the first time that the cause of Christ could actually demand his life's blood, as it had the Stams'. Confronted with that reality, he was ready to surrender and concede defeat.

"How can I remain on the field?" he asked himself. "I would be living in defeat. How can I preach victory when I have lost the battle?"

But as the questions of staying flowed through his mind, the problem of going home drowned all other thoughts.

"What of the money people have invested in sending me to China? How will I explain why I left so suddenly? How can I go home in such obvious failure? But if I stay I will be nothing less than a hypocrite." The questions unrelentingly stormed his mind, and he could find no peace.

But God was not ready to let his young soldier surrender. There was much ahead for this man, and China was only the beginning.

In God's providence, that same day, nearly 12,000 miles away in Pasadena, California, a little woman was sleeping peacefully in her modest suburban home. Suddenly, at midnight, she awakened, as though an unseen hand had shaken her. As she lay there, she became aware that someone was in need of prayer. She tried to brush aside the conviction that she ought to get up and pray.

After all, she thought, *I have been faithful in my prayer time each morning.*

The urge to pray increased. She obeyed the prompting of the Holy Spirit and, switching on the light, knelt down by her bedside. As she prayed through her prayer list, she came to the name of a young man who had been in China less than two years. She had never met him but had seen his picture in a missionary magazine and had faithfully prayed for him each day. Now she felt a strong burden for him. Was he in some physical danger? Or was he facing some spiritual conflict? She did not know. But in the intensity of her burden for him all she could do was cry, "Dear God, see him through, see him through—"

As he knelt in a mud-walled hut in faraway China, the battle raged in Dick's discouraged heart. Then, after nearly two hours of agony, a strange quietness settled upon his restless soul. In the stillness, the One who had promised to go with him and never leave him gave him a very simple but straight message: "Don't doubt Me. I will see you through. . . . I will see you through."

In the darkness of midnight a woman in Pasadena prayed. At that very hour in far-off China God took away the darkness and spiritual disaster that overwhelmed a defeated soldier. God unlocked the heavens, and defeat was turned into victory.

6

The Day the Dog Died

Kong was twenty-two and a respected teacher in the Honan district where Dick lived and worked. Among the Chinese he was distinguished by the fact that he had finished eight years of school and was certified as an elementary teacher.

At school he read a Bible for the first time. He devoured the Old Testament in just a few months and read quickly on into the New Testament. In the tenth chapter of the gospel of John he met the Good Shepherd.

Kong knew all about shepherding. He had tended his mother's small herd of goats before school. He understood Christ's parable. He wanted to know this Shepherd intimately.

One Sunday, after a seven-mile hike to the mission church, Kong was introduced to the Shepherd and began to follow Him.

When Dick arrived in Shenkiu, Kong was the natural choice as his language teacher and traveling companion. Always the traditional Chinese gentleman, Dick soon dubbed his new friend "Little Confucius," meaning "Teacher Kong."

But it was soon apparent that Kong could teach Dick much more than just the characters in the Chinese language, more than tone and pronunciation in the sing-song dialect of the Honan people. Kong could teach Dick much about a true childlike faith that pleases God.

His simple faith was unquestioning. He accepted God's promises without doubt or hesitation. His deep faith startled Dick out of what could be called a "Yes, but—" mentality.

Dick remembered saying those words back in college. *"Yes,* Lord, I understand You mean China, *but* the language—"

Moses had said it. *"Yes,* Lord, I hear You. *But* my mouth—"

And the Chinese villagers of the Honan district were no different from Dick or Moses. The religion of the foreign missionaries required that they destroy their idols and stop burning incense to their ancestors. The consequences of such drastic action terrified them.

The new teachings of the strange, fair-skinned man and his friend Kong demanded that they let go of the tightly clutched practices and superstitions that were familiar—familiar, though confusing and condemning as well. Their religion was a mixture of Taoism, Confucianism, and Buddhism and contained no revelation of Jesus Christ.

"Yes, but," they asked, "if we burn our idols and worship the Supreme Emperor in heaven, who will placate the evil spirits? And if we do not burn incense for our ancestors, who will say prayers for us when we die?"

Kong attempted to explain the gospel, or happy news, in simple terms that the villagers could understand. But the happy news required a costly break from the traditions and customs that had bound centuries of Chinese culture.

Always their response was, "Yes, but—"

Kong sympathized with the reluctance of his people to let go of their long-held religious practices. He too had once been in bondage to fear. But his fear had been replaced by faith. And he longed for his people to learn of this faith and to experience the freedom he now enjoyed in Jesus. It was a longing that he and Dick shared; a longing that urged them to make the dusty hikes each week, from village to village, sharing the happy news wherever there were people who would listen.

During one such preaching trip through the villages, as Dick and Kong took turns explaining the happy news, the crowd surrounding began to grow agitated. Whispers and murmurs disrupted the carefully planned sermon Dick was trying to deliver. He could see he was beginning to lose his audience.

"Now what have I done?" he wondered to himself, recalling the time he had preached an entire sermon about a pig coming down from heaven—the words *pig* and *Lord* being similar. Had he again misused a word or phrase, causing his listeners to turn their interest elsewhere?

His confidence seeped from him, and he turned to Kong with a helpless gesture. *Help me,* his eyes pled with his teacher-friend.

Quickly catching sight of his friend's distress, Little Confucius stood up to politely restore silence when he was interrupted by a piercing scream.

"*Chiuming* (save life)!"

The scream came from the doorway of a house down the street. The entire crowd, including Kong and Dick, rushed across the cobbles of the road toward the house. As they ran, Kong overheard someone in the crowd say that the spirits had arrived and a man was possessed.

"That is heathen superstition," Dick cautioned Kong.

"But Pastor, the Bible tells us that in Jesus' time men were possessed. Could not the same thing happen today?"

Dick started to answer Kong, but stopped. *Could it?* he asked himself.

Crowding into a small courtyard they could hear the sounds of struggling in the house, and they strained to see what was happening. Just then a distraught woman pushed her way through the villagers and came to Kong.

"The people say that you trust in the Supreme Emperor of heaven. I beg you to ask Him to help me! An evil spirit has again possessed the father of my children and is trying to kill him," she pleaded, her face distorted with fear.

Dick could hardly believe what he was hearing. With Kong in the lead, they moved through the crowd toward the thatched hut where the afflicted man was. They stepped over a mangy brown and white dog that partially blocked the doorway and followed the little woman into a sparsely furnished mud-walled room.

When his eyes adjusted to the dim light of a peanut oil lamp, on the bed Dick saw a middle-aged man held down by four other men. Although the prone man could not move his legs or arms, he was tossing his head wildly from side to side. Blood slowly oozed from a deep gash in his forehead—a wound, they later learned, that had been self-inflicted.

The atmosphere of the room seemed charged with evil, so real and close Dick felt he could lift his hand and touch it. His skin prickled with fear.

Little Confucius sized up the situation swiftly. He addressed the family of the struggling man. "An evil spirit has possessed Farmer Ho. Our God, the 'Nothing-He-Cannot-Do One,' is bigger and more powerful than any spirit, and He can deliver this man. First, you must promise me you will burn your idols and trust in Jesus, the Son of this Supreme Emperor."

An old woman who was praying before the ancestral tablet in the corner raised her head in surprise, but no one spoke. Finally, one of the men nodded his assent.

Then, turning to the young missionary Kong said, "You will sing with me three verses of the hymn 'There Is Power in the Blood.'"

Dick thought, *Yes, I believe that, but—*

Before he had time to question, Dick heard Kong's voice and he joined his own to the not-so-pleasant sound of his teacher.

"Would you be free from your burden of sin?
Would you o'er evil a victory win?
There's power in the blood,
Power in the blood . . . "

Wonderful power! As the words to the song filled the room Dick could feel the atmosphere begin to grow calmer. Farmer Ho's writhing and struggling eased.

As they sang the last line of the hymn, 2 Corinthians 10:4 flashed into Dick's mind. "For the weapons of our warfare are not carnal, but mighty through God to the pulling down of strong holds." For the first time he knew he was experiencing the forceful meaning of this verse.

There in that little mud-walled hut he and Kong were fighting a spiritual battle such as they had never fought before. Swiftly, quietly, Dick named each part of the "armor of God" and slipped it on by faith.

Kong reached out and took hold of Dick's hand. "Now," he said, "in the name of Jesus we will command the evil spirit to leave this man."

Dick clutched Kong's hand tightly and tried to swallow down the uncertainty that was rising within him. Kong straightened his shoulders and began to pray boldly, fervently, that every member of the Ho family would turn to God and away from the idols and be saved.

He had just begun to pray when the dog screeched and yelped. Dick turned and saw the poor animal whirling in circles snapping wildly at his tail. Kong never paused, never missed a word, but kept right on praying. Dick and the Ho family gazed in amazement as the dog suddenly fell over—dead!

Sudden silence dropped into the room.

Dick stood transfixed, staring at the dog, and a picture from another time and place filled his mind. He could see Jesus commanding devils to leave a man. He could see the account in the gospel of Luke: "Then went the devils out of the man, and entered into the swine: and the herd ran violently down a steep place into the lake, and were choked" (Luke 8:33).

Kong had finished praying, and Farmer Ho was quiet and relaxed. The family was instructed to fix the resting man some chicken broth. While the wife set about preparing the meal Kong began to teach the family more about Jesus.

Two weeks later, the Ho family burned their idols and their ancestral tablet and became Christians. When Mr. Ho was baptized he testified, "I was possessed by an evil spirit who boasted he had already killed five people and was going to kill me. He would have accomplished his boast, but God sent Mr. Kong along just at the right moment, and in Jesus' name I was set free."

7

From Farmers to Fishermen

Dick once said, "God didn't take me to China for what I could do for China, but for what China could do for me." This was especially true during the earliest years of his ministry.

Through the long hours of struggle with the language he learned the real meaning of the word *determination*. The attacks of loneliness that occurred so regularly sent him seeking deeper intimacy with God. He gleaned fresh insight into God's promises of constant presence and friendship. As he grew more aware of his own weakness, the strength of the God who had called him became more real each day.

But even with all the evidence of God's blessing and power, Dick was troubled and often depressed.

Each day he viewed the vast countryside with its myriad small homes. Everywhere the eye could see, small brown huts peppered the landscape. The tiny shelters, thatched and mud-walled to insulate against the cold of winter and the heat of summer, nestled close to the wheat fields that supported a way of life that had seen little change in recent centuries.

One and a half million Chinese! How could one man reach them all with the gospel, the happy news? The impossibility of his task overwhelmed him.

The salvation of the Ho family had been a great thrill to both Dick and Kong. It had been a dramatic lesson of trust and victory. But that family was only one of the vast number of families drawing their existence from the fertile fields of the Honan's agricultural regions.

Including the Ho family, there were only a few dozen Christians in the entire area. And they knew nothing about preaching. The demands of their small farms and large families made it hard to expect them to help with this impossible mission. That left the task to Dick and his budding evangelist, Mr. Kong.

Together they trudged the plains of the Honan's inland territories, stopping to preach wherever and whenever there were groups of people.

As Dick entered the marketplaces of the villages, curious dark eyes in small faces pressed around him. The novelty of his fair skin and blue eyes acted like a magnet to the crowds that filled the market. News traveled fast that a foreigner was in the village. Within a short time a sizeable group gathered to listen to this strange-looking man with round eyes. And when he began to play his trumpet, even those less curious folks milling in the streets could not resist giving him their attention.

Though he was still inexperienced, Dick knew enough to keep his messages simple.

Often he began by drawing the crowd's attention to the ancient Chinese character for *come*. The symbol is made of a cross with two little men hanging on the ends of its outstretched arms. In the center hangs a larger man. Using this aid, it was not difficult to explain the meaning of the crucifixion.

"This is the Savior's invitation to you," he told his listeners. " 'Come unto me, all ye that labor and are heavy laden, and I will give you rest.' "

Surely these hardworking farmers can understand this verse, he told himself, and watched their faces for some sign of comprehension.

But he soon used up all his Chinese vocabulary and then turned over the preaching to young Kong. Kong, with his understanding of his people's superstitions and fears, tried to lead his listeners toward the One True God and away from the idols and false gods. But few responded. Few believed. All too few.

What was wrong? Futility and exhaustion began to eat away at Dick. The multitudes of the Honan regions would never be reached at this rate. Where had he gone wrong? What was withholding the blessing he had expected God to pour down on his ministry?

The Ho family was an exciting victory—an example of what God *could* do in the lives of these people. But for each success story there should be hundreds more! It was too slow a process. It would be years, even decades, before the Word reached all the people of this region. How many would die without Christ in that space of time? Something had to be done.

Long nights found Dick awake and miserable, fighting off the greedy, whining mosquitoes that found their way through the netting draped over his hard cot. The little mud-walled hut was stuffy and airless, and seemed especially dark and hot as he tossed and turned, struggling with his thoughts, unable to sleep.

Then one sleepless night, as Dick's thoughts wandered through familiar Bible passages, one verse seemed to stand out from all the rest. Lying in the dark, staring at the blackness of his walls, a light seemed to come on in his mind.

"And He said unto them, Follow me, and I will make you fishers of men" (Matthew 4:19).

The twelve disciples followed Jesus everywhere! They learned from Him how to preach, how to reach out to the multitudes, how to feed the hungry the Bread of Life. There was no one following Dick! His message was right, but could it be that his method was all wrong?

This was a new and exciting possibility! Dick sat up and exclaimed aloud, "I could duplicate the method of Christ!"

Suddenly all desire for sleep fled. He pushed aside his mosquito net, lit the little peanut oil lamp and opened his Bible to the book of Acts, the first chapter.

"Ye shall be witnesses." It was Jesus speaking to the disciples gathered around Him at His ascension. But could he also be speaking to the handful of Christians in Shenkiu? The farmers, the merchants, and the housewives?

Dick read on in the book of Acts and discovered that Paul the apostle also used this method of evangelism.

It was suddenly so clear. He had been trying to evangelize the world by himself. Resolve followed realization. He determined to make some changes in the days ahead.

The next Sunday morning in the little Shenkiu chapel his text was Acts 1:8, "Ye shall be witnesses."

"Brothers," he addressed the Christian farmers in his congregation, "please stay behind after the service. I have something very important to discuss with you."

At the close of his sermon the farmers gathered around him. "Harvesting will be completed in several weeks. Then you will have nearly a month of free time before you can plant your next crop," he told them. "During your slack time I want you all to go out into the villages and witness with me."

Mr. Ma interrupted excitedly, "But Pastor Hillis, how can I preach when I have only a third-grade education?"

"You can read," Dick answered him, "and as a Christian farmer you can tell unbelieving farmers what Jesus Christ means to you."

Then the questions came fast.

"But if we are gone for a month what will we eat?"

"How much will you pay us?"

"We don't even know how to witness. How can we learn?"

"One at a time!" Dick laughed. "We will eat the same things you would eat at home, but we will carry it with us. As for salary, well, turn to your Bibles and if you can find how much Jesus paid Peter and John, I will give you the same amount! You will learn to witness by following me."

The farmers were skeptical, but they agreed to give it a try. They closed with a short prayer meeting and a promise to meet again on the last Monday in October, when the harvest was finished.

In spite of their doubts, the Christians who gathered at the little church that Monday were eager to begin their training as witnesses for Christ. Each one brought with him a sack of flour or a basket of soy beans to be used as food staples for the month. No sleeping bags were necessary, as the men slept on straw spread on the mud floor of the church.

For the next month they followed a disciplined schedule. Every day at 5:00 A.M. they pulled on their long quilted gowns and cotton wadded trousers and took time for individual prayer and Bible study. At seven they breakfasted on steaming hot flour and water gruel, then they went back to Bible study and evangelism training. About 9:30 A.M., young Kong, the elected captain of the group, sent the men out two by two. Every day Dick accompanied a different team.

As they entered the village marketplaces Dick would let the Chinese Christians tell the great love story.

"Come and hear the good news," they would call.

"Down with your false gods and your idol worship. You worship the god of peace, and you and your mate fight like roosters. Is it not so? You worship the god of wealth, and has he made any of you rich? Are you not almost starving to death? You worship the goddess of health, and sickness walks in and out of your front door. I urge you to turn to Jesus!"

"Who is this Jesus?" the villagers wondered. "How do you turn to Him, and what happens if you do? And what is good about this news? Nothing these strangers from Shenkiu say sounds very good!"

At dusk each day the teams returned to the church to rest hoarse throats and tired bodies and to share the experiences of the day. At first their experiences were not very encouraging. When Dick's turn to speak came, he told the villagers very clearly of the life, miracles, death, and resurrection of Christ, but the Christians with him seemed slow to realize that *their* preaching contained no good news.

Then came a cry from a man called Mr. Lin.

"Please come to my home and help me burn my idols! I want to become a Christian."

The cry was addressed to another Chinese farmer, Mr. Ma. That was the day Mr. Ma finally saw the importance of preaching the Good News. As the simple story of God's grace unfolded from his lips, the Spirit of God revealed to Mr. Lin his need of the Savior.

"You must help me find the true God," he begged.

He had no way of knowing the fear and excitement his request raised in Mr. Ma's heart, and the rejoicing in Dick's!

Mr. Ma and Mr. Chang, his teammate, went home with Mr. Lin and explained to the family God's great love for them, God's great gift to them, Jesus Christ.

"If you would worship the true God you must rid your home of the false," they told them.

Together they took down the ancestral tablet, two paper gods, a clay kitchen god, and an incense bowl. With an air of triumph the men carried the idols outside and smashed and burned them. Then the little family knelt in prayer with the two Chinese Christians.

When the teams gathered back at the church that night there was a festive spirit, a feeling of celebration over the faith of the Lin family.

Ma and Chang could not hide their enthusiasm. "The gospel is the power of God, even when *we* preach it!" they testified to the others.

Their enthusiasm was catching, and the little group of men suddenly saw that a farmer could win a farmer. Now the days were not long enough as the Christians discovered how readily the villagers would accept the Good News from their lips. Then the food supply ran out, so the team members returned to their homes and farms.

"But we will be back as soon as the sweet potatoes are harvested!" they promised. And they were as good as their word.

The gospel swept across the thickly populated country carried by farmers calling themselves the "Gospel Workers' Team." From village to village the Shenkiu Christians traveled, witnessing to their rural neighbors. Soon a similar women's team was born. In the next five years so many new churches were formed that the elders of the Shenkiu church went to different villages every Sunday so each new group of believers could hold the Communion service at least once a month.

Dick's excitement and enthusiasm swelled as he led the native believers, taught them the Word, and sent *them* out to do the work of evangelists. As he watched the power and success in ministry that resulted when he imitated the Master Teacher, Jesus, he became convinced that this is the way God intended to evangelize the world. Just as Christ mobilized the disciples, teaching them and going with them, so Dick and Kong did with the Christian villagers of Shenkiu.

The formula "every Christian a witness" enabled the Chinese believers to accomplish the impossible: to offer the Bread of Life to a huge and hungry population. This formula was the seed that germinated and grew into the philosophy that later became Overseas Crusades.

But the seed was first planted in the land of Honan, a distant agricultural region of inland China, an unlikely place to find farmers turned into a crew of fishermen.

8

Love Story

The trauma of unrequited love has been the story line of many a famous novel. It was a personal drama for Dick Hillis, even through the unfolding drama of God's grace toward him in the Honan. He was in love with a beautiful girl, and she was in love with his best friend.

Though his life was full of the many tasks and joys that are a missionary's, he was often plagued with emptiness. Though he had friendships with many of his Chinese countrymen, he still felt a deep loneliness. His days bulged with activity, yet he longed for something more. He longed for Margaret Humphrey.

Frustration washed over him each time her name and face came to his mind. The beautiful dark-haired girl with hazel eyes and gentle smile was an ocean away and yet as present as the fur-lined parka he pulled on each day. He could not remove her from his thoughts. And to further complicate the matter, she was only vaguely aware of his existence.

He had been only a few months into his relationship with Jesus Christ when love hit him. But the object of his love was soon going steady with his best friend.

Dick could not simply give up and look for someone else. *Why search elsewhere when you have already found what you want?* his heart said. But what he wanted was outside his reach.

Yet she continued to fill his thoughts and his prayers.

In the last hours before Dick's boat sailed for China he had still refused to give up. He recruited a trusted friend to act as a benign spy.

"Write me every six months," he instructed his friend. "Just tell me how she is, what she's doing, and—well, if she's still going steady."

For four years the letters arrived from America. Like clockwork the time ticked by in six-month increments, carrying the monotonous toll of "situation status quo."

Dick often reminded himself that Jacob of the Old Testament waited seven years for his bride. He wondered if the same would be asked of him. He had loved her throughout his years at Bible school. Now after four years in China he could not stop loving her. Yet he wondered, *Have I made a mistake? Am I clinging to a wild dream?*

Promises and proverbs jumbled in his mind as he sought his Bible for guidance, some kind of assurance, hope maybe, that God would give him Margaret for his wife.

"Hope deferred maketh the heart sick," he read in Proverbs. And then, "He that spared not his own son . . . how shall He not also freely give us all things?"

He was sure she was God's choice for him. Time could not erase her face from his mind, nor her name from his lips. His loneliness for her did not subside even in the face of his demanding work among the Honan's masses.

He ached for the companionship of Margaret Humphrey, for the joy of private jokes and whispered words, for the bliss of holding her in his arms. Yet even as he dreamed of her, reality infringed on his mind: she had probably given him little or no thought since he left for China nearly four years ago.

It was a very hot summer day when the Chinese postman handed him another "spy" letter. Dick opened it with very little anticipation. He knew by heart what it had to say. But as his eyes scanned the words, he suddenly caught his breath.

"They are no longer going together. Margaret feels that God wants her to serve in China. She has already applied to the China Inland Mission . . . has been accepted . . . and will sail in six months."

Before he reached the last sentence his legs felt like overcooked Chinese noodles. He dropped to his knees and prayed, "Thank you, God! If you will only get her safely to Shanghai, I'll do the rest!"

Then suddenly he remembered, *I have no reason to believe that she is interested in me!* And he asked himself, *What am I going to do? I can't go to Shanghai and meet her. I can't just leave my work and travel hundreds of miles to woo a girl I haven't seen for four years. What would the mission think? Oh, Lord, I will need Your help in this matter even after she arrives in Shanghai!*

He had no choice but to make his first move by letter. "Faint heart never won fair lady" goes the saying. So he mustered all his courage and put his heart in a letter that went something like this:

> For years I have loved you. I have prayed for you and want you to be my wife. You have not seen me for nearly five years, but we did know each other pretty well for the years we were in Bible school. You will say you can't accept my proposal without courtship. I have to answer that in our circumstances there can be no courtship until you have accepted my proposal. This is hard, I know, but it looks as if your decision must be based on God's will for your life. It is easy for me to believe that you are God's will for *my* life as I have already admitted my deep love for you. For you it is a much bigger problem, so I will gladly give you six months to answer me. This allows you time to really pray. God will show you His will, I know. Before I close, let me ask you a question. Did you come to China because you loved the Chinese or because you were sure this was God's will for you? I know your answer—you came because you knew it was His will. Knowing this, you are confident that He will give you His love for the Chinese. Will you, dear, let me relate this same clear logic to your decision? If it is His will for you to be my wife, then will He not give you a love for me? Margaret, I will be praying every day—many times every day—because I love you.

Margaret Humphrey arrived in Shanghai in October 1936. She had expected strange emotions and confusing experiences upon her arrival in a foreign country. The mission orientation classes had tried to prepare her for those. But nothing could have prepared her for the confused state of her feelings when she opened the letter that was waiting for her at the mission headquarters the day she arrived.

She stared at the signature at the bottom of the letter. *Dick Hillis.* Her forehead creased in puzzlement. She remembered him from her Bible institute days as a good-looking young man known for his outgoing personality and unusual energy.

"But I haven't given him more than a fleeting thought since he left for China!" she mused in amazement. Letting her mind rove back over the years she recalled his more than passing interest in her during their years together at Biola.

But even then, she thought, *I felt nothing more than friendship toward him.* And now this—a marriage proposal! She was baffled and more than a little shocked.

Margaret had had her share of marriage proposals in the recent years. But she had refused to let anything or anyone interfere with her desire to serve

God as a missionary in China. After graduation from Biola, she attended the University of Washington. Then she applied to and was accepted by the China Inland Mission.

Now she had arrived in China full of confidence that she was finally embarking on her life's work. But her confidence changed into confusion as she regarded the letter from Dick Hillis. *What am I going to do,* she asked herself. *What am I going to do?*

In honesty she had to say she did not love him. She admired him and had enjoyed his company on the few occasions they had been together. But after four years in China he could be a completely different person. And, like any other young woman, she had her own dreams of someday experiencing "great love." Was she to lay that aside in order to marry a man who was, in many ways, a stranger to her?

She could make no decision at the moment. She needed time. Would six months be enough, she wondered, to determine if this man she had not seen in four years was the man God had chosen to be her husband?

"Lord," she prayed, "You have guided me this far. I will trust You to lead me into the decision that will glorify You!"

Margaret was determined to tell no one about the marriage proposal she had received from the young missionary living in the Honan province. She would pray about it alone and wait to see the direction God would lead.

On one of her first days in Shanghai, a missionary lady invited her to tea, and for no apparent reason, the conversation turned toward the subject of marriage.

"I met my husband only once," the veteran missionary told Margaret, "before he proposed to me. I prayed about it and felt God was telling me to accept."

Margaret sat forward on her seat, her attention riveted on the woman whose face was filled with peaceful joy.

"We were married not long after that," she continued. "God has blessed our marriage with true love that has grown deeper through the years."

Margaret wondered at the time why she had been selected to hear this story of the woman's unusual marriage. She was soon treated to another moment that caused her to wonder. She paid a visit to one of her former Biola professors who was teaching in China for a year.

"Margaret," the woman said, "I have been praying for quite some time that God would bring you and Dick Hillis together."

Margaret was shocked. No one knew of the letter containing the proposal. No one knew of the searching that was going on in her mind as she daily prayed and considered what God would have her do about Dick Hillis.

The prayers of this saintly woman are usually answered, she thought, and trepidation filled her.

Within a few short days the mission sent Margaret to the China Inland Mission's Women's Language School in the city of Yangchow. She was busy from dawn to late evening, studying the language, becoming acquainted with China's complex culture, and learning to know her missionary classmates. She had little time to do more than daily pray about Dick's proposal and carry on a weekly correspondence with him.

Through his letters she came to know him as a direct and definitely appealing young man. She was soon looking forward to his letters and often found herself storing up bits and pieces of her life that she wanted to send to him in her next letter.

In March she learned that she could not put her decision off much longer. The mission director was due to arrive soon to appoint each of the new missionaries to their stations. They would be scattered all over China.

Unless she told the director that she had future plans including a certain young missionary in Honan, Margaret might find herself sent to a distant southwestern or northwestern province for a seven-year term. That would no doubt rule out any possibility of marriage to Dick.

Yet still she wrestled alone with the question. How was she to decide God's will? She recalled God's guidance in the past, how he had used little signs along the way to lead her to Biola, to the University of Washington, and then to China. Did it mean something that God had called her to the same country as Dick, to the same mission organization, and that Dick had waited for her all these years?

She prayed and waited, and as the six months came to an end, she knew she had come to a decision. A deep inner assurance filled her. She knew that marriage to Dick Hillis was God's plan for her life. There could be no doubting it. She was certain.

Before Dick received her letter saying yes, she told the mission director that God wanted her to go to the Honan province and become Mrs. Dick Hillis.

Though the decision was made, and though she could not doubt the rightness of that decision, there was a measure of fear in her mind.

"Lord, I'm not afraid of doing Your will," she confided in her prayers, "but I am afraid of the unknown. And so much of my future husband is unknown to me."

Dick's letters did much to remove the fear from Margaret's mind. They were full of all the love and exuberance of a young bridegroom-to-be. And Margaret began to sense a responsive love for him growing in her own heart once she said yes to God.

The wedding plans took form through the letters that traveled between them. The ceremony was scheduled to take place in Hankow, central China, in six months.

Six months! Dick thought. *It's too long.* And yet, six months didn't seem so long compared to the six years he had already waited for the love of the woman of his dreams.

*H*igh school graduation.
Monroe, Washington, 1930.

*D*on and Dick, 1932.
Dick went to China in 1933,
Don to India in 1936.

China, 1933.
Dick and friends at language school
cut each other's hair.

Shenkiu, Honan.
Dick in Chinese dress. Hudson
Taylor said, "In everything not sinful
become Chinese that you might win
Chinese."

Dick with fellow
evangelist Mr. Kong in Honan, 1935.
Kong means Confucianist. He was
the sixty-sixth generation from Confucius.

Dick and Margaret's
wedding picture, 1938.

*W*elcome received on
return from their honeymoon.

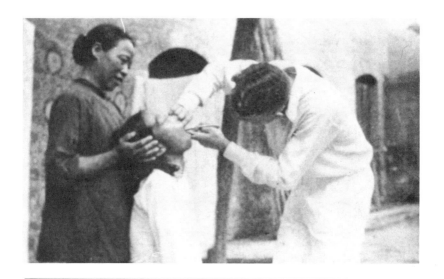

Dick would talk
about Christ while pulling teeth.
"They couldn't argue with you while
your hand was in their mouth."

Margaret with John
and Margaret Ann at the time
of Dick's appendicitis attack.

Dick preaching
to a crowd.

Dick's favorite
mode of transportation.
He wore out five bicycles
while in China.

With Chinese
church leaders.

*T*he Hillis Family
in 1950. (L to R) Margaret Ann, Dick
holding Jennifer, Margaret holding
Brian, Nancy. Steve and John in
front.

*D*ick (kneeling L),
Uri Chandler (L), and Ells Culver (R)
made up the first team to Taiwan.
Here they are joined by Roy Robert-
son (center) and Dawson Trotman of
the Navigators (kneeling R).

Dick Hillis.

"Being confident of this very thing,
that he which hath begun a good
work in you will perform it until the
day of Jesus Christ" (Philippians 1:6).

9

Shadow of Death

On April 8, 1938, Dick Hillis and Margaret Humphrey were married. The wedding was much different from that of Margaret's girlhood fantasy. The crowded church she had dreamed of was exchanged for a small parlor in a tiny mission home in Hankow. Instead of the white flowing gown she had imagined, she wore a simple suit. There were no banks of fragrant flowers, but a thoughtful Chinese friend gave her a small bouquet of azaleas. The gathering was made up of well-wishers, but her closest friends and relatives were an ocean away in America.

There was no wedding music—only the percussion effects of Japanese war planes bombing a distant part of the city. Japan's assault on China was escalating, and the reverberating sounds of war accompanied the little ceremony held in the mission home.

After a short honeymoon, the couple traveled up to the drab little city of Shenkiu. It was there that Margaret would join Dick in his work among the Honan farmers.

Their home was an old mud-brick house. It was far different from the white cottage of the young bride's dreams. It boasted a rickety veranda, families of rats, and, according to the old Chinese dowager who sold it to them, the ghost of her deceased husband. This last bit of information made it possible for the mission to afford the house—the old woman was anxious to be rid of it and its haunting spirit.

Margaret learned quickly what missionary life was like. She joined Dick in the work among the Chinese Christians, leading the women in Bible studies and teaching the children. And each day brought the challenge of language study as well.

Her housekeeping chores were complicated. The dilapidated house had no running water, no electricity, and no plumbing. Paper windows allowed only sparse light by which to do the household tasks.

Working together in the isolated region of the Honan province, Dick and Margaret found their love for each other growing steadily. The years since their first tennis match had changed them both, and they knew they faced a time of getting reacquainted. Yet a sweet intimacy and spontaneous friendship developed quickly.

The first seven months of their marriage passed in a hurry as life for the newlyweds settled into a pattern. Then out of nowhere Margaret was struck by a devastating fever.

There was no doctor; the nearest hospital was one hundred miles away, and there was no adequate transportation. Dick stood helpless and desperate. Though he prayed, he found no answer.

"Why, why?" his mind cried out. "Why doesn't God answer? He couldn't take her from me. He knows I need her, not just for myself, but for the work also. A man can't work among the Chinese women!"

He dropped to his knees beside the bed, and his hand grasped her hot, dry one. As he knelt there his mind went back to a long letter his father had written to him before his marriage. One phrase burned into his heart: "Remember, Dick, if you are really in love, you will face the danger of loving the gift more than the giver."

Deep conviction began to pierce his heart.

"Oh, God, You have given me so much to love in Margaret. Is it possible that I have loved her too much?" he asked, and the answer to his question shone clear in his mind.

"Little children, keep yourselves from idols." It was a harsh truth to admit, but was it possible that he had allowed his beloved to become his idol?

Dick bowed his head with real contrition. "Lord, I give Margaret back to You. If You require it of me, I will walk to her grave, still trusting You. But if You will raise her up, I will always seek to put You first."

Peace filled him, and for a short while, he was able to rest. He was certain he would find her temperature down by the next morning. But daylight showed no improvement. Margaret still burned under the heat of a 105-degree fever.

*I must trust—I must believe—*he told himself. *He that spared not His own Son—*The words tumbled through his mind. And as he prayed again, the thought came that he should go down to the Chinese herb shop.

The dried-up old medicine seller greeted him warmly but refused to be hurried. "Tell me the disease, and I will find you a cure," he assured Dick.

"My wife has a fever, a high temperature, and, well, I don't really know what is wrong!"

The old man rubbed his beard. "I regret that I can do nothing for you."

Dick started the walk back to the house, but he had not gone far before he heard a young lad calling him, "Pastor, the medicine seller wants to see you again."

He hurried back to the shop to find the old man standing in the doorway holding a small glass vial. "Honorable pastor, two years ago a traveling medicine man sold this to me. I don't know what kind of medicine it is, but the man said it will cure any kind of fever. You can have it for sixty-six cents if you want it."

"*If* I—of course, I want it!" Dick took the vial from the old man's hands and hastily examined the label. The words were in German. Could God have sent a small vial of medicine all the way from Germany to this little Chinese town for just such a time as this?

He hurried home and gave Margaret an injection of the medicine. In the middle of the night he heard a weak call for water—a good sign! She took only a sip, but Dick was encouraged. At daylight her temperature was 104 degrees. By noon it was down another full point. In two weeks Margaret was the same as if she had never been sick.

Years later Dick would say, "I have never been the same. I have learned that I dare not put the gift ahead of the Giver. Since then, both gift and the Giver have become more wonderful to me."

10

Handwriting of God

The wedding music of Japanese bombers was only the prelude to the strife and terror that accompanied the next several years Dick and Margaret shared. In 1937, the Japanese began a full-scale invasion into China. The cacophony of war beat toward a crescendo.

The explosion of bombs, the roaring drone of war planes, the thudding footfalls of approaching enemy armies, the stacatto of guns—all these became familiar sounds, terrifying sounds that reverberated through China's countryside.

By January, 1941, the Japanese army had penetrated deep into the inland provinces of China and was approaching Shenkiu. Each day it drew closer to the little mud-bricked house and the family of four that lived there. Dick and Margaret, now the parents of two small children, knew there was little they could do to protect their little ones, little they could do to protect themselves.

Eyes strained toward the horizon, in constant search for the dreaded enemy. Villagers listened intently for the warning sounds that would send them scurrying for safety.

Constant reports on the position of the advancing Japanese soldiers kept Shenkiu's inhabitants tense and uncertain. The presence of nationalist troops nearby brought comfort, but with it came the knowledge that their city would be the scene of intense fighting once the enemy arrived.

As the invading soldiers drew closer and closer to the Hillises, trouble from another sector erupted.

Dick was jarred out of a restless, troubled sleep in the middle of the night. Sharp pains tore through his abdomen, doubling him over, taking away his breath.

Oh, please, he thought, _it can't be appendicitis._ But the pain stabbed again, and with it came the other symptoms he knew to be related to appendicitis. He needed a doctor, but there was none in Shenkiu. As the knowledge of what he must do dawned on him, dread and fear joined his pain.

He would have to make the long and painful trip to the nearest mission hospital by ricksha. There was no other choice. Only a doctor could diagnose and treat his illness, and operate if necessary. But the trip to the hospital meant leaving Margaret and the children alone to face the onslaught of the Japanese troops moving steadily closer by the minute.

Dick gritted his teeth against the pain as he bounced along the rutted, war-mangled paths in the ricksha. As his physical discomfort increased, his fear for his family intensified.

As Dick journeyed the 115 miles to the mission hospital, Margaret made her own journey of faith. She noted the calendar on the wall: January 15. It would be days—weeks, possibly—before she would know of Dick's condition. She knew there was little she could do but wait and pray.

She took a deep breath to steady herself, turned into her kitchen, and forced herself to concentrate on the tasks that awaited her. There was milk to boil, work to be done. Perhaps the time would pass more quickly if she kept her mind and hands busy with the mundane essentials of her household.

Just then the gatekeeper at the mission compound limped into the kitchen doorway, bowed crookedly, and announced, "Pastor's wife, here is his excellency, the colonel."

Margaret had only a moment to wonder what message the commanding officer of the defending Nationalist troops could be bringing her.

The colonel entered briskly and announced, "The enemy is advancing into Honan Province, and we have orders not to defend this city. For your own safety, you should find refuge in one of the villages away from the city."

Margaret bowed politely. "Thank you for your gracious concern for an unworthy woman, sir."

As the colonel departed, the icy January wind swept through the small room. Suddenly the enormity of her danger overwhelmed Margaret. She was alone in a war-threatened Chinese village, totally responsible for the safety of their two children, year-old Johnny and two-month-old Margaret Anne.

She looked at the little daily scripture calendar nailed to the kitchen wall. Again she thought of how long it would be before she could expect Dick to return. He could be away until the middle of February.

How can I ever manage without him? she thought. The decisions ahead of her would determine the life or death of her babies.

By mid-afternoon the army garrison in the little city was empty. The soldiers' departure created panic. Families packed their goods and fled.

The church elders called on Margaret before they left. "Come with us," they pleaded. "We will care for you while Pastor Hillis is away."

Margaret looked at the concern in their eyes and thought of the country homes to which they were headed. She loved these people, but she knew their village huts held death for Western babies. The many tiny graves in the mission compound proved the danger.

Yet how could she explain without offense that she could not take her children into the unheated, mud-floored huts where three and four generations crowded together? Just a few weeks earlier the six-month-old son of the nearest American family had died of the dreaded dysentery.

No, her babies would stay near her own kitchen where she could boil milk and water and where one room was always kept warm.

She could not tell the Chinese friends these reasons. Bowing, Margaret thanked the village Christians for their concern but said she'd wait for her husband's return and watch over the mission property. That night she went to bed shaking with fear.

Would the hardened soldiers of the imperial army attack during the night?

When little Johnny awoke whimpering in the cold, Margaret took him to bed with her and lay awake a long time, listening to the wind rattle the waxed-paper window panes and praying that her little boy would live to see his daddy again.

Early the next morning, Margaret hurried to the kitchen to start the water boiling for Margaret Anne's bottle. Automatically she reached up to the wall calendar and tore off yesterday's date. The Scripture verse for the new day gleamed like sunlight: "What time I am afraid, I will trust in thee" (Psalm 56:3).

Well, I certainly am afraid, Margaret admitted to herself. *I fulfill that part of the verse! Now indeed is the time to trust God.* Somehow God's promise sustained her through that tense day.

The city was being evacuated rapidly. Other church members came to invite Margaret to their country huts. But the Scripture held the young mother. She was not to panic but to trust.

By mid-morning the next day the city was nearly deserted. Then the compound gatekeeper came to Margaret, his eyes blurred with fear. "I must leave," he said. "Please, Pastor's wife, come take refuge with me in my village beyond the city."

Margaret hesitated. The deserted city would be an open invitation to bandits and looters. What would she do without the protection of the gatekeeper? But the risk to her babies in the village huts was certain; in the city she faced only unknown fears.

She declined the gatekeeper's offer and watched him as he took his leave apologetically.

It was noon before Margaret remembered to pull the page off the little daily calendar on the wall. The Scripture for the day read, "And they that know Thy name will put their trust in Thee: for Thou, Lord, hast not forsaken them that seek Thee" (Psalm 9:10).

As Margaret bowed her head over the noon meal, she poured out her gratitude to God for those particular words at that moment.

Her main concern now was food. Fresh meat and produce were no longer coming in daily from the outlying farms, and all shops in town were boarded shut. Although the goats that provided the babies' milk were still in the compound, the man who milked them had left for his village. Tomorrow Margaret would have to milk them herself. She wondered if she could ever make the balky little beasts hold still.

Margaret slept uneasily that night, worrying about how she would feed her children and sure of very little except that she should stay in the city and somehow trust God.

The next morning she was awakened by the sound of distant gunfire. The Japanese must be advancing toward the city. She knew that she must milk the goats before the actual shelling began and goats became frightened and unmanageable.

Margaret decided that before she faced those goats she had better fortify herself with a bowl of rice gruel and with the new day's Scripture promise. She tore the old page from the calendar and God's Word to her was, "I will nourish you, and your little ones" (Genesis 50:21).

The timeliness of these daily verses was becoming uncanny. With some curiosity Margaret examined the back of the calendar pad. It had been put together in England the year before, but God in His all-knowing love had provided the very words she needed a year later—on the other side of the world.

Margaret was still eating the gruel when a woman suddenly stepped into the kitchen, carrying a pail of steaming goat's milk.

"May I stay and help you?" she asked, holding up the pail. "See, I have milked your goats."

Diminutive Mrs. Lee had been a neighbor for years, but that morning Margaret felt that she had been sent from heaven. Mrs. Lee explained that she had no family living and that she wished to show her gratitude to the mission by staying in the city with Margaret.

Through the long day, the two women cared for the babies and listened to the noises of the approaching battle. Late in the day, a loud rapping at the gate set the women's hearts pounding. Mrs. Lee went to open it. Her face beaming, she ushered in the caller.

"Gee-tze! Gee-dan!" she cried triumphantly. "Chicken! Eggs!"

A frail, black-robed country woman came in with a live chicken and a basket of eggs. "Peace, peace," she said, giving the customary Christian greeting as she bobbed shyly. Noise of the cannons had not kept her away when she remembered the missionaries would be hungry.

God had fulfilled the promise on the calendar. He had seen to it that the little ones were nourished! That night Margaret's heart was full of hope. While shells burst over the city she prayed that somehow God would spare Shenkiu and these gentle people.

Next morning, Margaret rushed down to the little square of paper hanging on its nail and tore off the page: "When I cry unto Thee, then shall mine enemies turn back: this I know; for God is for me" (Psalm 56:9).

Was it too much to believe this time? Margaret pondered. Surely it couldn't be right to take literally a verse chosen just by chance for an English calendar?

As the gunfire drew closer, Margaret and Mrs. Lee began to prepare the house for invasion. Any papers that might possibly be construed to have military or political significance had to be hidden or destroyed, so the women searched the desk and church buildings and burned papers that might be misunderstood.

By nightfall, the gunfire sounded from both sides of the city. The women went to bed dressed, prepared at any moment to meet the Japanese invaders.

Margaret awoke abruptly in the early dawn and strained her ears for the crunch of military boots on gravel. But only a deep stillness surrounded her. There were no tramping feet, no shrieking shells or pounding guns, only the waking murmur of little Johnny in his crib.

Misgivings warred with excitement as Margaret woke Mrs. Lee. The women went to the gatehouse, each carrying a child. Mrs. Lee was the first to stick out a cautious head.

"There is no one in the street," she told Margaret. "Shall we go out?"

The women stepped through the gate and watched as the streets began to fill, but not with Japanese soldiers. The townspeople were returning from their country hiding places. Had the Chinese won?

As if in answer to the unspoken question, the colonel stepped up. "Pastor's wife," he said with relief, "I have been concerned about you!"

Then he told Margaret that the Japanese had withdrawn. No, they had not been defeated. Nor could anyone arrive at a reasonable conjecture concerning their retreat. The enemy had simply turned back.

Margaret stepped into her kitchen, eyes fixed on a little block of paper pinned to the wall, and sent silent thanksgiving to the God who is enough.

11

Strange Angels

More than a hundred miles away from Shenkiu, on the snow-covered plains of Honan, Dick huddled in his ricksha. The pullers slowed to a stop along the side of the war-rutted road and stooped down to rest. Dick grimaced as pain tore through his side. *Only a little farther,* he thought, praying he would be able to endure the remaining miles to the hospital.

His thoughts of Margaret and the children brought him another kind of agony. *If only this hadn't happened to me now,* he thought, and wondered what was happening to his family at that moment.

The slow journey was made even more miserable for him by freezing temperatures. His fur-lined robe did little to shield him from the cold, but he hugged it closer around him as the pullers picked up their load and resumed the journey. As they topped a rise of land overlooking their destination they paused to gaze at the sky in disbelief.

Japanese war planes were bombing the city. From their vantage point Dick and his party watched the destruction. The sky burned yellow and red as tongues of flame licked the horizon. As they stood watching, dazed and unbelieving, a bomb explosion ripped through the hospital buildings. Dick gasped as he saw the flames consume his only hope of relief.

When the droning sound of the bombers faded away, the little group inched toward the town. Miraculously Dick found a doctor in the rubble and confusion of the ravaged city. But the only help he could offer was in the form of advice.

"Yes, Mr. Hillis, your illness is appendicitis. But I can't do anything for you here. You will have to go to the hospital in Shanghai," he said.

Dick could see he had no other choice. But he was determined to return to Shenkiu first, to take Margaret and the children with him.

The thought of crossing again the 115 miles of bitter cold, war-threatened countryside he had just covered brought him a shudder of dread. And thoughts of what he might find when he arrived back in Shenkiu were unbearable.

"Please, Father," he cried silently, "let me find my family safe and unharmed. Please, Father."

With each step of the journey the Holy Spirit seemed to remind him, "Nothing is yours. Your wife and children are merely loaned to you. They are to be used for God's glory. Nothing is yours."

The constant pain in his side punctuated the truth. Even life itself was not his. Should the appendix burst he would be buried in a shallow grave on the Honan plain.

As he traveled back the slow, agonizing distance through the sub-freezing winds he prayed continually.

Days later, as the ricksha pulled into the mission compound Dick's face lit up with astonishment. The villagers were bustling about Shenkiu, tending to their normal activities as though death had never stalked their walls. He could find no words to express his relief and joy at finding Margaret and the children well cared for and safe. Yet the urgent pain in his side reminded him that danger was still very close.

He knew his condition was critical. He could waste no time getting to a hospital.

"It will be a long, arduous trek, Margaret; hard enough for a healthy man, but for a sick man, a woman, and two babies, it could be torture." Dick's eyes held the concern he felt as he tried to prepare his wife for the ordeal that lay ahead for them.

Margaret packed suitcases with the things they would need for the journey. As soon as Dick had rested they loaded everything into two rickshas. Christian pullers promised to take them as far as they could.

Just before they left they bowed their heads. "Lord," Margaret prayed, "You know we need milk for our babies and men to open up doors—doors that will take us through the Chinese front lines, through no-man's land, and through the enemy's lines and on into Shanghai. Lord, let us learn the truth of Your promise 'The angel of the Lord encampeth around them that fear Him.'"

Then they settled into the rickshas. Little Margaret Anne snuggled close to her mother in one ricksha while Dick held baby John in the other. With the blankets and robes tucked in around them, they were ready. Margaret and Dick exchanged tentative smiles as the pullers picked up their burdens and stepped into a steady rhythmic pace.

The first day ended in discouraging defeat, for they had gone only a short distance when they were forced to turn back because of heavily falling snow. It was a cold, bleak house that gave shelter to the little family that night, and it was easy for their spirits to sink.

The next morning the snow had stopped falling, so once again they headed for the front lines. It was slow and tedious travel. On the evening of the second day they arrived at the headquarters of the defending Chinese army on the southern bank of the Sand River.

Dick went to see the commanding officer to request permission to cross the battle lines.

"Fool!" bellowed the commander. "You are crazy! The Japanese will attack at any moment, and it will mean certain death to step across the lines into no-man's land!"

Dick could see the officer was in an overhappy state through too much wine, but he persisted in his request for permission to cross the lines. And the commander persisted in his drunken shouting.

"Between here and the Japanese army there are groups of bandits. They are vicious! They are plundering anything and everything that was left behind by the villagers who have fled this territory. You are in worse danger from them than from the Japanese!"

The belligerent commander was sure such a description would discourage the strange American family that wanted to cross the windswept plains beyond the Sand River. But Dick was not easily dissuaded, and the officer finally gave in. He wrote the paper giving permission to cross the river and enter the war zone.

With the paper in his hand, Dick's next challenge was to find a place for his family to spend the night. It would not be a simple task to find a house in this little community that was already crowded with soldiers.

As he left the general's headquarters, the son of a fine Christian saw him. He recognized Dick instantly.

"Pastor Hillis," he greeted Dick. "Can I do something to help you?"

It was a strange offer coming from a young man who had refused to accept his father's faith. He had broken his father's heart with his life of wickedness and even now was engaged in smuggling opium across the lines.

Yet Dick was glad for any friendly interest, even if it came from a smuggler. He told the young man of his family's circumstances.

The youth led the family through the streets to a little mud lean-to. There were no doors or windows, but it was shelter. They put down their oilcloth, unwrapped their bedding, and ate a meager supper by the light of a peanut-oil lamp. Dick's earlier stop in the marketplace had provided steamed bread, sweet potatoes, and some hot flour-and-water gruel. With their hunger satisfied, they laid down and slept.

Just at daylight the next morning the smuggler led them to the edge of the river where they found a boat he had chartered for them. They were taken across the river and several miles into no-man's land. As the smuggler left them to return to his river headquarters, Dick and Margaret knew they had much to be thankful for: they were alive, and God had provided an angel in the form of a smuggler who had led them through many dangerous hours.

Once they left the boat and began their journey by ricksha again it was not easy to find their way. There were no roads. The dull February days saw no sun. But unseen angels seemed to lead them along the right path. At one point, when pain and exhaustion seemed too great to endure, Dick heard the voices of the faithful ricksha pullers as they broke out into a Chinese hymn taken from the gospel of John, chapter 14.

> "Let not your heart be troubled,
> Ye believe in God,
> Believe also in Me."

The progress across the desolate no-man's land was slow, too slow for a sick man. The miles of flat, snow-covered fields were dotted with small deserted villages. The people had fled west in their retreat from the Japanese. The doors and windows of their homes gaped open—an inviting paradise for plundering bandits.

The setting sun on the second evening across no-man's land found them tired, discouraged, and running out of both food and milk. As they stopped outside an abandoned house in a large deserted village, Dick wondered, as he had many times that day, "Do You see us, Lord? Do You have more angels for us?"

They carried their few things into the house and began to settle down for the night. Dick was on his knees rummaging through one of the suitcases when a rough voice behind him shouted, "*Chi-lai,* stand up!"

Even before he turned around Dick knew: *We have been captured by bandits.* He turned slowly and looked up. The guns he saw pointing at him confirmed his fears. He barely had a moment to draw a breath when the leader ordered his men to take the suitcases. Then in sharp, crisp barks, he demanded all of Dick's money.

Dick reached for his wallet and at the same time did what comes so naturally in China—he handed his namecard and asked, "What is your honorable name?"

The simple question angered the bandit.

Cursing, he demanded, "Do you want to be able to identify me to the authorities?"

Then, as suddenly as his rage had erupted, it subsided and a strange look came over his face. "Why, your name is the same as mine!" he exclaimed.

It was customary for a foreigner living in China to be given a Chinese name. Dick's language teacher had given him a very strange surname—one completely unused in that section of Honan, and in eight years in China he had never met anyone with that same name. Grasping at a straw, he said to him, "Kind sir, we are brothers, members of the same family! We are now united!"

"It is true," the bandit answered in a somber voice. "You are my elder brother."

Turning to his soldiers, he ordered them to return all of the goods they were holding and to see that everything was put back into place. He assured Dick he would do his duty, for Dick was his elder brother. He forgot the difference in their skin color and the national origin. They had the same surname, and that made them brothers. He ordered his men to unroll their blankets for sleep, and that night bandits and missionaries slept together.

Next morning, the "angel" provided his best man as a guide for Dick and Margaret's continued journey across no-man's land. That afternoon the guide left them within sight of the Great Walled City after showing them that just outside the city were the Japanese lines. Not certain just how to proceed from this point, the little party paused and committed themselves into God's care, and then moved cautiously forward toward the walls of the city.

Suddenly, two Japanese sentries stood before them and shouted something at them that they could not understand. Dick took off his hat, shouted back to them in English, and slowly walked up toward the pointed guns.

The soldiers began to search their rickshas and suitcases, jabbering at them in their unintelligible language. After a few minutes they moved behind the pullers, held bayonets to their backs, and ordered them to march up to the gate of the Great Walled City.

By this time the sun was setting and Dick and his family were tired, hungry, and feeling ill. They had prayed on the road that they might be able to get inside the city to a little church. There they might be able to spend a night in privacy, perhaps even be able to take a bath. But as they marched toward the city, aware of the bayonets against the backs of their faithful friends, the chances of such luxuries seemed remote. At the gate a battle of words began between the guards and the sentries who had captured them. The guards had been ordered to let no one inside the gate. They were adamant; they would not open the gate.

Suddenly the sound of galloping horses filled the air, and three Japanese officers rode up. The one in the center was a two-star general. In perfect English he addressed Dick. "Where in the world did you come from?" he asked.

Dick was astonished. Then quickly he answered with his story of illness and his need to get to a hospital. As he finished his account, he added wearily, "We need rest, baths, and milk, sir. And may I ask you, sir, where did you learn such perfect English?"

Without hesitation the officer informed them that he had attended the University of Washington in 1936.

"General," Dick said, "give me the pleasure of introducing to you one of your fellow alumnae. My wife was also at the University of Washington in 1936."

The general's face beamed with amazement and delight. He greeted Margaret warmly, promising to fulfill any requests he could. Margaret's first request was for a quiet place to rest and for milk for her babies. The general immediately barked some orders in Japanese to his men, then turned to his fellow alumna and promised, "You shall have all that you have requested. In the morning I will give you a pass to take you on through Japanese lines. You will find milk at the little church, for the former missionary there owned a cow."

The great gates creaked open to admit the exhausted company. The people of the city gawked at the dirty little party as they passed through the streets toward the Christian church. There the cow was milked, water was heated for baths, and they spent a restful night in the little mud and straw church. The next morning the general provided the promised pass and an escort to take them safely outside the city.

Standing there, with the walls behind them and miles still stretching in front of them, Dick knew the danger was not all past yet. How would the next city receive them?

Many hours later they approached the next big city, also Japanese-occupied. There was a small church in the suburb, but would the enemy troops allow them to remain there, or would they be forced to go on into the city? It was just after dark as they entered the outskirts of the suburb. There the harsh voices of guards challenged them.

"Who are you and where are you going?" came the question.

Dick answered in Chinese, "We are Christians. We are going to the little church right here in the suburb."

The darkness hid their identity, and the guards did not trouble to spot them with their flashlights. They were satisfied with Dick's perfect Chinese language. They never imagined he was a foreigner. He was given the password to proceed on into the suburb.

Soon they were welcomed into the little church. Much to their surprise they discovered that a foreign missionary was still living there. He had sent his family home as the Japanese moved toward his city, but he had determined to stay himself. Dick and Margaret and their company walked into his living room and were immediately enveloped in cozy comfort. A warm fire burned in the fireplace, electric lights glowed, and from a radio the "Old Fashioned Revival Hour" could be heard in the background. With a sense of nostalgia, Dick realized that it had been eight years since he had heard that broadcast.

Their host set about preparing beds, baths, and food for his unexpected guests. That night they slept as they had not slept for many nights. And when they awoke the next morning, the dawn was bright with hope.

The last leg of their journey was in sight: a train ride into Shanghai. Their new missionary friend escorted them to the train station. There they said tearful good-byes to the six pullers who had used the muscles of their bodies to pull them across the dangerous miles of hostile terrain to bring them to safety.

As he relaxed into the seat on the train, Dick closed his eyes and remembered with amazement the different "angels" God had sent in response to Margaret's trusting prayer at the beginning of their journey.

The train trip, though long and hazardous, brought them finally to Shanghai. Dick entered the hospital, was operated on immediately, and was soon on his way to recovery.

In the many years since the harrowing journey across the inland provinces of China to the port city of Shanghai, Dick has heard the words of the verse "The angel of the Lord encampeth around about them that fear Him." And an army of angel escorts parades before his mind's eye.

12

From Shanghai to San Francisco by Bicycle

It was an exhausted, war-weary family that returned to America for furlough soon after Dick's surgery. For the next four years, from 1941 to 1945, they were busy, yet strangely restless.

Dick studied at Dallas Seminary for a year. Then the family returned to Los Angeles where Dick served as professor of missions and director of practical work at his alma mater, the Bible Institute of Los Angeles. But he yearned to be active again in the practical work of missions himself. He was eager to get back to the land he loved, the land that had become his other home—China.

In 1945, at the conclusion of World War II, the China Inland Mission called for men to return to China to survey the condition of the Chinese church. Dick Hillis was among the first to volunteer.

It was to be a grueling survey assignment requiring at least five months of trekking across thousands of miles of Chinese countryside. It would mean a painful period of separation from his family. Though he dreaded the time he must spend away from Margaret and the children, he was anxious to see how his Christian brothers had come through the war. His task was to assess the damages and the victories in the lives of the Chinese believers.

Just before his ship pulled out of Seattle's harbor, some friends learned that Dick would need a bicycle. Aside from walking, that was the only means of transportation that could be used for the many miles to be covered during the survey. His friends graciously bought him one, but it was too late to send it on the ship he was taking. He left the States with the promise that his bicycle would be sent on the next ship leaving for the Orient.

Dick often wished that he could blot from his memory the trip from Seattle to Shanghai. The Pacific was stormy and rough and tossed the little freighter like a toy. The passengers celebrated Christmas on board, but no one was in a celebrating mood. The ship's cook prepared a delightful Christmas dinner, but eleven of the twelve passengers were too ill to eat it. Dick was one of the miserable eleven.

But the days of seasickness were worth the joy of being back in China, the land of his adoption. How good it was once again to use the Chinese language he loved so well. His pleasure at being "home" again was tainted only by the sight of the war's destruction.

The city of Shanghai bore cruel scars. One section of the city had been flattened by bombs. Starving beggars picked through the rubble and garbage. Everywhere he looked there was pain and suffering. The poverty of the city overwhelmed him with grief.

But he had to move on. His assignment was 450 miles northwest of Shanghai, and he still had to figure out how he was going to get there. Railroads had been bombed out; bridges were not yet rebuilt. There were no bus lines. It was impossible to walk from Shanghai to Honan.

Sitting in a hotel room in the ravaged city, Dick thought ruefully of the new bike somewhere out on the Pacific. It would have been the perfect answer to his problem. But he could not spare the time to wait for it.

For several days he prayed and searched for the answer to his problem. One afternoon he went to the Australian embassy to see a missionary friend who was temporarily holding the office of Australian ambassador. In the course of their conversation Dick mentioned his difficulty. His friend was ready with a suggestion.

"General Chennault, the general who held off the Japanese air force during the war with a tiny group of brave airmen, has decided to stay in China," he told Dick. "With some Chinese friends he has established the first commercial airline in the country. He calls it the Civil Air Transport—CAT for short. One of his planes might be flying out your way. Why don't you go see the general about it?"

Dick's visit with the general—a man with a weather-beaten face and kind eyes—was a pleasant one, for he was sympathetic to the work of the missionaries. He informed Dick that many Japanese were still armed, even though the surrender papers had been written.

"Your trip is bound to be filled with excitement, maybe even with danger," he warned. "But I know you are determined to go, so let me offer you a ride in one of our planes that is leaving in three days for the city of Kaifung—free of charge, of course."

It was an unforgettable trip. Dick was the only passenger in the bucket seat of the DC-3. He spent the time watching the Chinese landscape below, the flat farmlands covered with clean white snow, and thought, *How much better this is than riding a bike!*

Kaifung, capital of Honan province, was a welcome sight. Dick loved the Honan people and their customs. The agricultural region had been his home for eight years, and he was glad to be back among the farmers and villagers he had missed for four years.

In Kaifung Dick was joined by two companions, Louis Gaussen and Henry Guiness. Together their purpose was to visit every major church in the province to find out the property damage they had suffered. As they surveyed the area, they planned to encourage the Christians to continue boldly in their witness for Christ and in their fellowship together. Unfortunately, there was only one bicycle among the three men. It was decided that the leader, Mr. Gaussen, would ride and Henry and Dick would walk. Once more Dick thought of his brand-new bicycle that was probably nearing the coast of China by this time. In his most frustrated and footsore moments, he couldn't help wondering if God hadn't made a mistake with His timing.

In spite of the blisters, the months of survey work were filled with joy. They found that many of the mud huts that served as churches had been destroyed, but they also discovered the Christians had remained true. War and famine had not tarnished their faith, but had polished it.

In one village a middle-aged elder greeted the men. "My entire family was killed during the war, but I know they are in heaven, and I will be with them again some day. Until that day I will be faithful to my God, even unto death!"

At every Christian home they were warmly welcomed and asked eagerly when the missionaries were coming back. They promised to return and live among them as soon as they could bring their families. After about five months of traveling, the three men arrived back in Shanghai with a report for the mission headquarters.

When they reached the port city, Dick found the new bicycle, still resting in its wooden crate. He ran his hands over its shiny chrome and looked sadly down at the worn-out spots in his shoes.

"Lord," he said questioningly, "this bicycle could have been such a helpful companion during the last five months. Now I have no use for it. Has the loving thoughtfulness of Christian friends been wasted?"

A few days later, on a Sunday evening, the CIM workers gathered together around the wheezy pump organ in the mission headquarters to sing. Besides the little handful of missionaries, several businessmen and an American colonel were there. During testimony time, Dick stood up to express to the group his thankfulness for the goodness of God. He told them of the endurance of the Chinese Christians and of their desire for the missionaries to come back. As he closed, he mentioned his plans to return to the States immediately and bring his family back to China.

Following the meeting, one of the missionaries hurried over to him and said, "Dick, from the way you talked in your testimony you must be counting on returning to the States in a matter of days."

"I'd make it hours if I could," Dick assured him.

He looked at Dick rather strangely. "Don't you realize there are literally hundreds of people waiting to get to the States? Shipping is impossible. There aren't any ships apart from military ships, and civilians can't get on those. You could be delayed for a mighty long time."

Dick was stunned. He hadn't had the slightest notion such a situation existed. As he tried to settle his agitation, the American colonel approached him.

"Did I understand you to say you were leaving for the States this week? How do you plan to make the trip?"

"Well, sir," Dick answered sheepishly, "I gave that testimony in innocence and also in ignorance, it seems. Up until a few moments ago I thought all I had to do to get home was to buy a ticket from a shipping company. Now I'm not sure what I'm doing or when I'm going."

The colonel assured him he would pray for him, and as he left he asked two questions.

"Mr. Hillis, how much luggage do you have?"

"Well, my Bible and a toothbrush are my only necessities," Dick answered with a laugh.

"And how soon could you be ready to go?" the colonel asked.

"Right now!"

The colonel stepped out into the street and was gone. There was no sleep for Dick that night. He couldn't control the frustration that kept welling up inside him.

"Before, when I needed a bicycle, I didn't have it. Now I have a bicycle, and what I need is a ship. Nothing seems to be at the right place at the right time, Lord," he complained as tiredness overtook him.

Next morning, while sitting down to a breakfast of boiled mush, he was called to the telephone. The colonel's voice boomed over the line. "There's a military transport leaving Shanghai for San Francisco this afternoon. If you can be ready, I'll try to get you on. The ship will be filled with military men, but I think I can make an exception for you. Now listen carefully and follow my instructions. First, go to the army barracks and get your shots. Then, go to the American President Lines ticket agent and buy a ticket. Next, go to the ship and you will find a stateroom that you will share with the officers. You will probably have to sign a statement saying as a civilian you are prepared to work on board ship, if necessary. Now get going, and God bless you, Mr. Hillis."

After this news, Dick had no taste for his breakfast. He hurried to his room, picked up his passport, and rushed to the military barracks. His enthusiasm was dampened a little when he saw a long line of men stripped to the waist waiting for the needles to be jabbed into both arms. He tried not to let his eyes rest on the long syringes as he stepped in line and moved up toward the doctor. His identity was questioned when the doctor noticed his civilian dress.

When he heard Dick's story, he decided, "We can't waste this stuff on you, mister. This is for the boys in the service. But I'll sign your slip for you."

"Thank you, Lord," Dick sighed a quick prayer. The first step had been easy and painless. He hurried back to the mission headquarters, his mind already concentrating on step number 2: buy a ticket at the American President Lines.

Back in his room he packed the few things he had and prayed. "Lord where am I going to get the money for a ticket? I've got twelve dollars in my pocket. That will never be enough. The ship lifts anchor in only a few hours. Lord, you will have to work this out for me. It's too big a problem for me."

Then he thought of his bicycle—his shiny new bicycle. Would anyone in Shanghai want to buy a bicycle? It had cost his friends only $35, but even that would help. He hurried down to question the mission business manager.

"Bicycles in Shanghai are very scarce now, Dick, because they weren't manufactured during the war. I am sure I could find someone to buy your bike. Leave it here with me and I'll see what I can do."

Encouraged, Dick then rushed to the office of the mission treasurer. He listened to the confused story and assured him, "It sounds good. Go on down and buy your ticket. We'll advance you the money. When the bicycle is sold, you can repay us. If it doesn't bring us enough money you can send us the rest."

Dick returned to his room and finished packing. His mind was filled with wonder as he thought about the events of the past few days.

While others have been waiting for months, I'm on my way in a day! he thought.

Suddenly the holes in his shoes and the blisters on his feet seemed not to matter. God had known what He was doing when He deprived him of the new bike for five months.

The ticket cost $110, and he rode home in luxury. The ten-day trip across the Pacific was fast and smooth and afforded Dick a much-needed time of rest and relaxation.

Word came later that a wealthy Chinese had wanted the bicycle so badly that he paid $350 for it—enough to take a man across the Pacific three times!

13

The Fraction of an Inch

In 1947 Dick fulfilled his promise to his Chinese brothers. He returned with his family to live in the Honan province of China.

The Hillis family had grown. Nancy and Stephen now joined older brother and sister, John and Margaret Anne. Journeying back over the ocean to China, Dick caught himself watching his children, thinking about his first voyage to China thirteen years earlier. He had been little more than a youngster himself then. *How things have changed,* he thought, as he saw himself as a husband, father, and now returning veteran missionary.

Questions filled his mind as he considered the China to which he was returning. During his months of survey for the mission he had observed and recorded the many obvious changes that the war years had wrought. But there were other changes that were undefinable; subtle changes that could be felt but not articulated. Grief was everywhere. A sense of distress pulsated in the atmosphere. What would their lives be like now in this saddened land that was tense with suspicion and unspoken fears?

Japan no longer threatened China. The attack on Pearl Harbor had brought the United States into the battle arena, and China gained allies against the tiny imperialistic island. When World War II ended with Japan's defeat, China relaxed her guard against her enemy neighbor. But another enemy stalked her from within. She was far from safe. Violent civil war raged within her borders.

While other nations laid down their weapons in honor of the armistice,

China's countrymen raised their swords against each other. Though other countries of the world finally knew peace, China only dreamed of peace.

China's long history is spattered with the blood of her many wars: wars fought against enemies from outside her boundaries and wars fought against enemies within. But the fight that now existed was of a different sort, and its consequences much greater. Geography was not the issue, but rather ideology. The aggressors' determined goal was to annihilate the very culture that was China.

Early stirrings of discontent came into being in 1921, with the birth of the Chinese Communist Party. Under Moscow's close supervision, the fledgling Marxist group grew strong. Soon its voice cried out for change.

But change would not come easily to a country like China. For twenty-five centuries Confucianism dominated Chinese thinking. The demand to throw out more than two thousand years of tradition and custom in favor of the new movement brought an adamant response of "Never!" from those who revered the old ways. But a growing number of intellectuals steadily sowed the seeds of revolution, and a Communist military force was established.

The Nationalist Chinese gathered strength and determined to defy their brothers. Chiang kai-Shek's leadership gave them courage and confidence.

Through the years intermittent fighting broke out between the two opposing ideologies. During those years there were brief periods of apparent unity between the Chinese. In 1937 they joined forces to withstand the marauding advances of the Japanese. But once World War II ended and the defeat of Japan was final, they again took up their stance against each other. No longer distracted by outside enemies, the battle for political supremacy in China became intense.

By the time Dick and Margaret arrived back in China with their children, the country was ripped into pieces by the angry fighting. Mao Tse-tung's communist troops were making steady progress across the plains of China.

China's ancient fabric of civilization was severely torn and hanging in pathetic shreds. There was no peace. There was no safety.

Knowing all those facts, Dick armed himself with a fresh assurance of God's sovereignty. He faced the prospect of life in China—his caution fringed with exhilaration at being "home" in the Honan province again. And he settled his family into the mission's brick house built on the banks of the Mule River in a village called Loho.

Dick's tongue rehearsed the Chinese words that he had had so little use for during the four years he had been back in America. It was good to feel the language in his mouth and hear its lyrical sounds again. His ears and eyes reveled in all the sights and sounds that had once been foreign to him, yet had become well loved.

He was glad to be back on the practical side of missions again. He walked through the cobbled streets of the village and preached to the crowds that gathered on market days. Thousands of farmers filled the town and spilled over into the neighboring countryside, displaying produce and sundry wares in the Mule River marketplace. Curious villagers paused to listen to the foreign missionary and sometimes accepted the offered pamphlets containing the "happy news" about Jesus Christ.

The mission church was located across the street from the Hillises' home. Every Sunday nearly a thousand Christians, many from surrounding villages, attended the worship services. Dick could hardly contain his excitement as he viewed the number of believers that filled the province. Farmers who had won farmers—he smiled to himself. Fishers of men.

Soldiers were a common sight in this market village. In peace times the Mule River Market was watched by only a small civilian guard. But this was a time of civil war. The market was now occupied by the Chinese Nationalist Army as protection against advancing hordes of communist troops.

When the Nationalists' Tenth Division arrived in Mule River Market, Dick struck up an unlikely friendship with the artillery captain. The handsome young Captain Hwang was proud of the little bit of English he could practice on the American missionary. But his greatest source of pride was his big gun.

Captain Hwang often boasted that the gun he so laboriously tended could lob a two-pound shell a mile and a half. He declared he could stop any Communist with it.

It wasn't long after his arrival in the Mule River Market village that he was able to put his boast to the test.

Early one December morning, Captain Hwang knocked on the front door of the Hillis home. Dick opened it and invited him in.

The captain began pacing the floor in an agitated manner. "Honorable Teacher, the Communists are marching on Mule River Market. It is possible they will reach the market by nightfall, and we will be in the midst of a hot war before the night is over!"

"What will be the outcome of the battle? Can you say, Captain?" Dick asked him, concerned for his family.

"You have nothing to fear. We can certainly take care of the Communists with our brave men and our big guns. But I think you had better take your family and flee. Although we will never retreat, we expect this to be a dangerous battle."

But is was impossible to flee. The Communists had blown up the railroad bridges both north and south of the village.

Just after 9:00 P.M. the Hillises heard the first shot, and all night the battle increased intensely around them. Sleep was impossible. The family spent much of that night in prayer. By midnight the battlefield had shifted closer. Shots whistled through the air as men ran from one building to another. In the darkness Nationalist soldiers could be seen on neighbors' roofs.

Though Dick kept reminding himself that Christ had promised, "I will never leave thee nor forsake thee," he found himself tightening into a tense knot. He fought to keep calm, but could hardly control his shaking.

Unknown to him, a tiny gate in the city wall had been opened by the defending general. While his rear guard was fighting a delaying action, he and his men were slipping out across the river to a great walled city just a mile away. By daylight all was quiet, and Dick knew that the brave Nationalist defenders had either surrendered or escaped.

When the sun rose he took his first peek out of an upstairs window. The street was filled with soldiers wearing red stars on their caps—soldiers of the Chinese communist army. How long before they would discover the Hillises? Would they torture or kill them as they had done to other missionaries not so long ago?

It was two days before the Reds discovered them. Dick and Margaret were surprised when they seemed to treat them with a certain amount of courtesy. The village teemed with fear and uncertainty. Margaret kept the children calm while she and Dick remained expectant, preparing for whatever their enemies might decide to do with them.

Yet their greatest danger lay not with the enemies, but with their young friend, Captain Hwang. His division lay across the river behind the walls of the big city to which they had escaped. The boastful captain apparently decided to remind the villagers that he still believed his big guns could defeat the Communists. He set up his artillery in his safe haven and began lobbing death into the streets of Loho. Unfortunately he was killing more civilians than Communists. But Dick could not tell him that. He could only pray that before the shells did any more damage he might tire of his deadly game of war.

As each shell dropped closer to their home, Dick and Margaret realized that they had to keep the children busy. To take their minds off the danger and noise they gathered them in the living room and suggested that they act out the famous Bible story of Esther.

John, the eight-year-old, was made King Ahasuerus. Nancy, the six-year-old, was voted the prettiest and paraded around as Queen Esther. Seven-year-old Margaret Anne volunteered to be the maid and set up the feast. Stephen, the youngest, was left with the assignment of portraying Haman. The play moved on with dignity, and the sensational hanging took place when King John used Daddy's tie to fasten luckless Stephen by his neck to the back of the chair.

As the children were performing this gruesome act, a shell exploded just two doors from their house. Dick turned to Margaret and said, "Keep the children busy. I'm going into the study to pray."

The words had scarcely left his mouth when the next shell exploded in their yard, driving glass, bricks, and dirt into the room where the children were playing. Dick shut his eyes in horror, expecting to find his children killed or injured when the dust cleared. But the next moment the four of them were clinging to Margaret and Dick, crying hysterically. The explosion had shaken and momentarily deafened them. They were covered with dust but unharmed. Not even a scratch could be found.

Dick gathered them, and together they hid in the little room under the stairway. Would the next shell hit them? Were they to meet death because of the act of a friend? He had little time to think. The next shell whined overhead and exploded in their neighbor's house, killing every member of the family. Brushing the tears from Nancy's eyes and the dust from her face, Dick tried to comfort her.

She looked up at her father and, still sobbing and shaking, said, "Daddy, I don't care if the next shell does hit us. Then we will go to heaven, and there aren't any shells in heaven."

Taking strength from the thought of heaven, he began to tell the children the story of Daniel.

"You know, we may meet Daniel tonight. John, what would you say to Daniel?"

John had been the first to stop crying. With remarkable control, he said, "I would tell him the same God who took care of him in the lion's den took care of us in the war!"

Suddenly there was quiet. Captain Hwang had finished his private war with the Communists. As the Hillises came out of their hiding place and looked at the room covered with bricks and sharp, death-dealing glass, Dick marveled that his children had come out of that room not only alive but without a scratch or a bruise. God must have sent His angels to protect His little ones.

That night they prepared their beds on the floor downstairs. The upstairs bedroom was too easy a target for Captain Hwang. They had much for which to be thankful—a supper of soup, a floor to sleep on, and after all, weren't they alive, uninjured, and together?

After the children were tucked in bed, Dick came around to pray with each of them. As he knelt beside Margaret Anne, he noticed a piece of paper tucked by her pillow. On that dirty scrap of paper was printed, in first-grade manner, "God is our refuge and strength, a very present help in trouble." Little Margaret Anne was sleeping on a very big promise from a very big God. Whether friends or enemies were shooting at her, her confidence was in God.

The next morning Dick examined the gaping hole made by the shell. Had Captain Hwang's big gun been raised a fraction of an inch, the shell would have exploded in the middle of the room in which the children were playing. That would have brought death to the entire family. *Not only are the hairs of our heads numbered,* Dick thought, *but the very fraction of an inch is determined by Him who said, "Fear thou not; for I am with thee: be not dismayed; for I am thy God: I will strengthen thee; yea, I will help thee; yea, I will uphold thee with the right hand of my righteousness"* (Isaiah 41:10).

14

The Longest Night

The Hillis family was just sitting down to their evening meal when a sudden bang on the door startled them. Dick was not surprised at the sight of the soldiers standing in the dim light of his kitchen doorway.

Such intrusions into their home were almost routine now that Loho was occupied by the Communist army. Since the Tenth Division had run from the city in defeat, they had become accustomed to their home's being invaded by Red soldiers at any and all times of the night or day. For weeks now, the soldiers had burst in, searched through personal items, rummaged through cupboards, and plagued the family.

The children, seated at the kitchen table, only glanced up from their meal and then went on eating. They were little disturbed by the latest intrusion. But suddenly Margaret stiffened with an intuitive awareness of new danger.

"You will come with me immediately!" the lieutenant ordered. Ten heavily-armed soldiers backed up the order. Dick had no question of their intent if he refused to obey.

"The general wants to see you at once," the lieutenant barked from the doorway.

"Don't be in a hurry, sir," Dick replied politely. "You are just in time for supper. Please step inside, and my wife will give you a bowl of steaming hot soup."

The officer grunted a refusal, and Dick tried again. "Tell your worthy general that it is almost dark and I cannot leave my wife and children now. I will come and see him in the morning, and he need not send soldiers to escort me."

"You will come with me immediately!" he commanded. "You have no time to finish your supper."

Dick turned for a quick look at his wife and children. Margaret was expecting their fifth child. *What will happen to them?* he wondered. *Could this be our last moment together?* Then he turned and walked into the night with his guards.

The children went on with their supper and Margaret began her vigil of prayer.

Dick walked through the streets of Loho flanked on either side by armed soldiers. When they arrived at the military headquarters the lieutenant left him outside with two guards and went in to report to his superiors. Through the half-opened door of the mud brick house Dick could see one officer sitting behind a desk writing. Several other officers sat on a bench smoking and talking. Were they the judges of his fate?

As he stood between the armed guards, the cold winter penetrated his coat and he began to shiver, both from cold and the fear within his heart.

Dick had good reason to be afraid. The Communists had executed three missionaries in recent months. It would not be hard to find a reason to kill him as well.

He gave himself a gruff shake to try and stop the miserable trembling, but instead only succeeded in drawing the verbal abuse of his two armed guards.

God, help me, he prayed. And verses of assurance began to flood his mind. *God hath not given me a spirit of fear,* he reminded himself. *If this fear is not from God, then I refuse it and accept only the things He gives: 'power . . . love . . . and a sound mind.'*

He began to relax as he was reassured by the promise that "all power is given unto me, and lo, I am with you alway."

God would take care of his family, he knew. And God would strengthen him and enable him to meet his accusers.

In the next moment the guards pushed him roughly through the small doorway to stand before the man who had the authority to snuff out his life.

"How long have you been in the service of your state department, and how much do they pay you?" the interrogator snapped.

"Sir, I am not a military or political agent of my government. I am a preacher of the gospel," he answered slowly. Weariness was beginning to mix with fear.

"When does the American army plan to attack China?"

"I do not know the political or military intentions of my country. I am a preacher of the gospel—" and so on through the many hours of the night. Many times during that endless night he wondered just exactly what he was accused of. One of the questioning officers kept returning to the subject of the little electric generator he had "uncovered" in the mission compound.

"But it was right in plain sight," Dick reminded him.

He brushed away Dick's words with an accusation, "You are an agent for the Nationalists, and with that generator you send messages to the enemies of the Chinese people."

"I will return to the house with you and start the generator for you," Dick offered. "I challenge you to send a message anyplace with it."

Perhaps, thought Dick, his crime was that of being a minister of the Christian gospel. He knew the Communists had spies in all the church meetings. They especially hated the doctrine of the second coming, and only yesterday Dick's text had been John 14:3, "I will come again, and receive you unto myself." Loho's Christians, facing persecution and perhaps death, had become excited about the hope of Christ's soon return. Maybe this had angered the Communists.

Or perhaps they had discovered the army uniforms down in the old well. They had been there for weeks now, ever since the night of the final battle between the Communists and the Nationalists over the little city. Two of the Nationalist rear guards used the mission house roof as their sniper position, and the Communists had outflanked them, making escape impossible. The two soldiers came to Dick in desperation. Their weapons were gone, and the Communists would execute them immediately if they were caught.

From the 170 Christian refugees crowded into the mission compound Dick obtained civilian black trousers and jackets. Now the two soldier boys looked like any other farmer or merchant. But what was he to do with the military uniforms? He hurried to the deep covered well in the corner of the courtyard, threw in the uniforms, and prayed they would sink.

The next day when he shone his flashlight into the well, to his dismay he discovered that the uniforms were only half submerged. To make matters worse, someone had thrown a military telephone into the well. Had the Communists found the phone and the uniforms? If so, Dick's fate was certain. He would never see his family on earth again.

Or perhaps he was being tried over the incident with the wheat. Several days after the city was captured, the Hillises had their third official search, or "inspection," as the Communists called it. This time a two-star general led the inspection party. He was greatly excited when he found two tons of wheat stacked in the Hillises' basement.

"I must have this for my army," he had demanded.

"But sir," Dick explained, "this belongs to the refugees who are living with us. When they had to flee from the battle zone they brought wheat to feed their families. If I give it to you they would starve, and your war of liberation would lose great face."

The general acknowledged the truth of that statement, but it was easy to see he was unhappy. Was this trial his revenge for Dick's thwarting his plans?

Maybe he was suspected of being a spy because of the rifles found on the mission compound. Less than a week after the fall of the city, the communist political agent made one of his frequent inspection tours of the compound. "What's that large pile of sand and gravel in the corner?" he questioned Dick.

"We had planned to build a room there," Dick said, "but the war has delayed the work."

"It looks suspicious to me," he said.

Dick decided to call his bluff. "If you question my honesty, I will ask some of the Christian refugees to move the dirt and prove to you that we are not trying to hide anything."

So the Christians set to work with shovels and wheelbarrows while the agent continued his inspection. Only minutes later Elder Tu slipped up to Dick and whispered, "We have found two guns buried under the gravel!"

Dick gasped. The guns must belong to the two soldiers he had befriended. This was excuse enough to shoot him on the spot or perhaps later in the town square as an example to the people. He made a quick decision. "Bring the guns to me."

Then, with an earnest prayer directed upward, Dick handed the guns over to the inspector, declaring his ignorance of the weapons.

He was never to know exactly what his interrogators were thinking throughout that long night. But Dick noticed that they too began to grow weary. Nine hours after Dick left his family the questions grew less forceful, less vindictive. After he had denied the charges of espionage for perhaps the hundredth time, Dick's ordeal was over as suddenly as it started.

"You may go home now," the superior officer directed with an expressionless face. "We have decided to let you live."

"Go home . . . let you live"—he'd never heard such wonderful words.

Not knowing the communist passwords, Dick knew he would be shot the first time he was challenged, so with good reason he insisted that a guard escort him home. As he made his way all too slowly through the semidarkness of the deserted streets, his heart and mind raced ahead to his wife and children.

Margaret met him as he flung open the front door. He pulled her into his arms and hugged her tightly.

"I prayed until about two," she told him, "and then suddenly the peace of God came over me and I knew you would be back. God gave me peace and so I slept."

15

One Mile Farther

Snow covered the muddy streets of Loho Christmas night 1947, and the Prince of Peace seemed far away. It had been only weeks since the shelling of the Hillis home by the proud young Captain Hwang and Dick's mock trial. Communist soldiers posed a constant threat to the believers in the village. All was not calm, all was not bright.

Dick lay awake at 2:00 A.M. fully clothed and alert to every sound coming from the streets. In the darkness he confessed to Margaret he couldn't help having the "shakes." God's miracles had protected them since the city of Loho had fallen to the Red soldiers, but who knew what the next day might bring?

Suddenly Dick was startled by a loud banging at the door—made by the butt of a gun. Slowly he rose, took a deep breath, and walked downstairs to the door. As he unlocked it, a soldier pushed by him, followed by eleven of his men in disciplined file. The leader marched to the center of the room and swung around to pierce Dick with flinty, cold eyes.

The lieutenant was about five feet eight inches tall and very thin. His uniform was filthy and hung loosely from his bony stooped shoulders. His small stature contrasted sharply with the ferocity and strength of his penetrating stare.

"Where does your wife sleep?" He seemed to spit out the question.

"Upstairs," Dick replied.

"Tell her I'm using her bed—she can sleep on the floor."

"You can't do this," Dick tried to bluff. "I'm an American citizen. This is my house, and I order you to leave!"

The officer's hand went to his hip and drew out a revolver. "Get out!" he ordered, his gun punctuating his command with authority.

Another night of bloody fighting had given the Communists firm control of the Mule River, a vital link between Peking, the capital of China, and the ancient industrial city of Hankow. Swarming hordes of communist soldiers flooded the tiny town of Loho and searched for temporary barracks. The mission home, on the southern bank of the river, made it ideal for the Red army's purposes.

Dick and Margaret grabbed the belongings they could carry and wakened the children. Hurriedly they crossed the mission compound to the uncertain safety of the little church nearby. A crowded congregation of Chinese Christian refugees already living there welcomed the Hillis family.

Twenty-eight days later Dick again saw the young lieutenant with the piercing eyes, this time at his invitation. He told Dick that within the week he would be leaving and he could have the house back. He assured Dick that he would find everything as he had left it, for his men were honest and devoted Communists. Nothing would be stolen. As he talked his eyes seemed softer, so Dick ventured a few questions.

"You say you are leaving next week. Where are you going?"

"That is a military secret."

"How long have you been a Communist?"

"Two years."

Knowing the strength of family ties in China, he then asked, "How long have you been away from home?"

"Fourteen months."

"And how old are you, sir?"

"Nineteen years old."

In China one is reckoned a year old when born, so that made him just eighteen.

"What do your parents do?"

"They are farmers in Shantung province."

"That worthy province was liberated by the Communists two years ago. I suppose your poor parents have received extra land and are better off now?"

"Not yet, but wait—the revolution is not over," he replied proudly. Dick's questions had not even ruffled his confidence.

Four days later at dusk, the lieutenant again sent for Dick. Oddly, Dick felt afraid as he said good-bye to Margaret and walked across the street to the house they had once called their own.

The sight left him speechless. Lined up in perfect order were the soldiers who had been living in the mission house. The young lieutenant was searching their pockets. On the ground lay an old toothbrush, a tube of medical ointment (one of the men thought he had a new kind of toothpaste!), and a used razor.

As Dick watched, the lieutenant pulled a fork from the pocket of the soldier he was searching, slapped him across the face, and said, "We don't steal!"

When the inspection was over, he picked up the things and gave them to Dick, apologizing that his men had dared to steal. Then he ordered Dick to look through the house. It was filthy, but not a thing was missing. There was pride in his voice as he said, "I told you nothing would be stolen. Now go get your family because we are leaving tonight."

"Sir, may I ask you where you are going?"

He answered by pointing to the high, ancient walls of a city one mile away. Dick couldn't believe it.

"Do you realize there are ten thousand well-armed Nationalist soldiers there?"

"Yes," he replied. "Our intelligence knows all the figures."

"How many men in your group?" Dick asked him.

"We have nearly five thousand men who will take part in the attack," he answered.

"How many of them are armed, sir?"

"Two out of every three."

"You have a formidable enemy behind walls thirty feet high and fourteen feet thick," Dick told him. "Your enemy is not only well armed but also protected by a deep moat. You have only half the number of men. To attack that city is certain death."

As he listened, the young lieutenant straightened up and his eyes flashed fire. "We will take that city tonight or die trying."

"But sir, has Communism done anything for you? What have you gained that would make you willing to lay down your life to carry it just one mile farther?"

"I fight not for personal gain," he replied fiercely. "It is what the world will gain that counts. I and my men are willing to die, if need be, but Communism must win. The rule of my life is 'Communism for all and my all for Communism'—and 'all' includes death."

With that he swung on his heel, gave a sharp command, and he and his men disappeared into the night. Standing in the darkness, Dick asked himself, "Mr. Ambassador, you are an American with a great Christian heritage. Would you be willing to die to carry your message just one mile farther?"

The move back into the mission house was a simple one. By ten that night the children were asleep. It felt good to be back in their home. Shortly after they lay down for what they hoped would be a night of good rest, a terrific explosion blasted away their sleep. Dick lit a match and saw by his watch it was 2:30 A.M. The explosion had touched off the battle for the adjacent city. Nothing blocked their view of the city where the battle raged, sporadically lighted by the flashing of bursting shells. The sounds of death and pain tore the night.

With the rising of the sun the firing ceased and men could be seen bearing the wounded on improvised stretchers. Dick and Margaret wondered if the Communists had captured the city. It didn't seem possible. Had the lieutenant who had been willing to die for Communism survived?

At 8:00 A.M. the remnants of the Red army retreated. That afternoon the commanding general of the Nationalists came over to see the Hillises. He was amazed that, in spite of the occupation of the Communists and the battles that had raged around them for the last several weeks, they were alive and unharmed.

Dick took him through the house and showed him where Captain Hwang's shell weeks earlier had hit the living room and had come close to killing them all. The general shook his head in wonder. He listened as Dick described to him the young communist lieutenant.

"Do you know anything about his company? They attacked the east gate," Dick told him.

"They didn't have a chance," he answered. "We had blown up the bridge across the moat. The Reds put down their scaling ladders and tried to crawl across, and we mowed them down like clay pigeons with our machine guns. The wounded drowned—it was a slaughter. Not a man of that company escaped."

"Not a man escaped." Though the fierce battle had brought temporary quiet to the area, Dick felt no peace that night. The words haunted him. In the moonlight he paced back and forth in the little yard of the mission compound. The communist officer, now dead, spoke to him: "I'll die, if need be, to carry Communism one mile farther."

Since 1933 Dick had been telling the great nation of China with its 400 million people that Christ revealed God's way of life and peace and salvation. The communist lieutenant, fiery and dedicated, had also proclaimed a message: freedom from oppression through a people's government. He had been terribly deceived, but God had used him to teach Dick that he must have the urgency, the conviction, the dedication that would make him a willing sacrifice for success.

In the moonlight, Dick bowed his head and prayed, "Oh, God, make me willing to live, and die, if need be, to carry Your message of salvation one mile farther."

16

The Jeep That Couldn't Be Stolen

The Hillis family had a chance to escape now that the Communist company had been defeated at Yenching. It was now or never. They had to leave immediately if they were to make it to Kaifeng, the capital of Honan, before Red troops stormed the plains to reclaim the province.

Every day that they waited increased their risk of capture or death at the hands of the enemy. With each new conquest the Communist armies grew bolder, more confident. The ferocity of their attacks grew more and more feared by the foreigners in the country who were regarded as spies. Their deaths were viewed as essential for the advancement of the revolution.

Word had been reported, mistakenly, that Dick had been captured by the Communists. The report was relayed to the mission headquarters in Shanghai. But by the time the report reached America, the broadcasters were saying that the entire Hillis family had been massacred. Though the report was false, further delay could make the news true.

But their exit from Loho would be no easy task. A 115-mile journey lay between them and Kaifeng, the provincial capital, a journey that had to be made by jeep. They had only enough gas for thirty miles at the most.

Dick and Margaret knew they had no choice but to pray and trust God to supply them with the fuel they would need for the jeep. As Dick bowed his head to pray, he recalled all the miracles that had surrounded that little jeep since it came into his possession two years earlier.

The story of the jeep really began 10,000 miles away, in the Sierra mountains of California. A group of young businessmen had hiked up into the mountains that overlooked beautiful Hume Lake. Under a clear, starlit sky they brought their burden for world evangelism before the Lord. They asked God to send forth laborers to the uttermost part of the earth, and they prayed for Dick Hillis, for his family, for transportation out to the field, and for transportation on the field.

That night, one of the young men, Dave, suggested that God might have a part for them in answering their own prayers. They couldn't go to China themselves, but with a little sacrifice they could provide a jeep for Dick to use in his work in the vast region of Honan.

A few weeks later the jeep stood in front of the Hillis home in Los Angeles. Dick promptly christened it "L.C."—the Lord's car.

The jeep was shipped to Shanghai when Dick and the family returned to China in 1947. Dick spent two weeks struggling through customs to get the jeep released to him. Each customs official gave him the same story: "I am sorry, but I cannot pass the jeep. It is illegal to bring a jeep into Shanghai."

As his frustration built, Dick decided his only recourse was to go to the top—the Customs Commissioner.

The commissioner received him courteously, and Dick could tell by the expression on his lean, tired face, that he was sympathetic to his cause.

"Sir, now you have heard my story," Dick said, after he had recounted his experiences with the other customs officials. "Would you kindly sign the papers that will allow me to go down and get the jeep from the wharf, please? This is the rainy season and the jeep has been sitting outside for three weeks."

"I am most sorry, but there is a new rule that no jeeps can be brought to Shanghai. The government will give you sixty days to ship your vehicle back to America. If you fail to do this we will be forced to confiscate it."

Although the commissioner kept sympathetically apologizing for his order, Dick was stunned by this turn of events. He knew there was nothing he could do. It looked as if the Chinese government would own the jeep.

The jeep was made a matter of prayer in one of the large missionary prayer meetings held in Shanghai. A young missionary happened to recount the story to a student friend of his whose father worked in the Bureau of Internal Revenue. A few weeks later Dick received a notice from the Customs Commissioner, informing him that the Bureau's new rendering of the law was that jeeps could not be brought into the country to be sold but could be kept for missionary work. His jeep was returned to him, and after the long journey 1,000 miles inland, for a year and a half Dick used it to travel across the plains of Honan.

Then one day, after the Marxists took Loho, a surly communist officer stepped into Dick's jeep and demanded the keys from his hand. The officer turned the key in the starter but the motor did not start. He jumped out of the jeep, jerked the hood up and peered into the engine.

"Na-ko tung'hsi tsai-na-li? [Where is that thing?]" he demanded, his hand moving to his revolver. The "thing" he wanted was the distributor.

"Excuse me, sir, I have it in my pocket."

Taking the distributor out of his pocket, Dick handed it over to him and he put it in place. In a moment he was back in the seat and the engine was running. How pleased the officer was with himself. And why not? He was the only man in town with a jeep. But it was Dick's jeep. Dick knew that the chances were not good that he would get it back. He tried to remind himself that it was the Lord's jeep. He had given it to the Hillises.

When the officer drove away, he didn't know that Dick had the key to the gas tank in his pocket. Sooner or later he would run out of gas and come back. Maybe then Dick would have a chance to reclaim the jeep. But Dick's weak faith argued that it would be difficult for even God to recover anything once the Communists claimed it as their own.

Several days later, Dick's son came running into the house shouting, "Daddy, Daddy, the jeep is coming back!"

The Chinese officer scowled angrily when Dick met him at the door. "Give me the gas key!" he commanded.

"That jeep is mine, sir," Dick dared to say. "You sign a paper saying you are borrowing the jeep, and I will give it to you."

The officer placed his hand on the gun holstered on his side and again demanded the key. Knowing this was no game he was playing, Dick handed him the key to the tank.

The officer left, and Dick's heart sank. He knew he would need the jeep if his family were ever to escape from communist territory. He struggled to believe that somehow they would be able to have the jeep back, but finally he gave up.

The children, however, seemed to see no reason to give up. Their prayers at the dinner table expressed their faith.

"Dear Lord," they prayed, "it is Your jeep. You loaned it to us. Daddy is the one to take care of it, but a man has stolen it from him. Dear Lord, You can do anything, so please bring it back."

The next Friday afternoon the officer returned, shaking and pale.

"Give me the ownership slip of the jeep," he demanded.

"But the jeep is mine, and I have no intention of giving it to you," Dick replied.

"If you will give me the pink slip, I will return the jeep at once."

Dick refused this request because he knew if the officer had the jeep and pink slip, he would have nothing to prove that he had ever owned the vehicle. The soldier's attitude changed, and he began to plead with Dick.

"You see, honorable sir, it is the pink slip for my life. The communist army has a rule that all military equipment captured must be reported immediately. The commanding general saw me riding around in a jeep, and he checked up on me. I hadn't reported the jeep, so I am up for court martial. Sir, I was so afraid, so I told them I had borrowed this car from a friend, a foreign friend. I told them this friend would give me proof—the pink slip. The tribunal said that I could have only six hours to produce this proof. Sir, they will shoot me outside the west gate in six hours! Please, sir, it is my life!"

Dick could see the agitated officer was telling the truth. It was a piece of paper for his life. He did the only thing he could do—he handed him the pink slip. As he left he promised, "You will have the jeep back in less than six hours. I wish I had never taken it!"

That afternoon the jeep was returned. As the family prayed around the table that evening, the children's hearts were bubbling over with thanksgiving. Once again God had unlocked the heavens and performed miracles. Dick had to make his personal confession to the Lord and ask him to forgive his unbelief.

With the jeep back in their possession and the Nationalist forces in control of their village again, they knew it was time to pack only their essentials and make their escape. But how far could they go on the amount of gas left in the tank of the jeep? Somehow God would have to provide the necessary fuel for their long journey. He had returned the jeep and had provided the opportunity for escape. Surely He would fill the tank with another miracle.

Margaret and Dick went upstairs to put the last-minute items into their suitcases when she clutched his sleeve. "Look, Dick," she said. "Lights coming across the plain. It must be a truck!"

As they watched the lights coming ever closer they wondered, *Is it a friend or an enemy? Is our escape to be blocked after all?* Fears and questions filled their minds as the vehicle drew close enough to be identified as a weapons carrier. It stopped in front of their house. They held their breath as they heard the truck door slam. And then a voice shouted in English, "Anyone home?"

In great excitement they opened the door to welcome two missionaries. As they fed the ravenous men some hot soup, one of the men, Henry, told them of the mistaken radio broadcast reporting the Hillises' massacre by the Communists.

"The missionary director in Kaifeng asked us to try to make contact with you—if you were still alive, that is," he told them.

"Alive and ready to make the journey to Kaifeng, but we do have one problem. Do you have any extra gas?" Dick asked.

"Sure, we put on four extra jerry cans of gasoline, enough to get you to Kaifeng. Don't worry about anything."

Again, God had answered before being asked. Dick was overwhelmed. If their rescuers had arrived just one week earlier they would have been captured by the Communist soldiers occupying the city. If they had come a day earlier, they might have been killed in the fierce battle.

As Dick had said perhaps a thousand times before, "Lord, I will never doubt You again."

17

The Final "Get Out!"

The journey to Kaifeng began early the next morning after much prayer and packing. The Hillises loaded their jeep, and at 5:00 A.M. they were ready to leave. The sleepy children curled up on top of the luggage, blissfully unaware of the danger into which they traveled.

It was true that the enemy had been defeated and the Nationalist army now controlled the near area. But the defeated troops that had retreated from Loho now waited between the Hillises and their destination. How would the young family avoid the Red army while traveling the distance to the great walled city that promised safety?

"Lord, let our missionaries get out unharmed. Blind the enemy so that they cannot see Your people," prayed the family's old Chinese cook as he said good-bye to his friends. His eyes were wet with tears as he watched the small jeep, heavy with its precious cargo, pull out of the mission compound and drive away.

All day they crept northward, keeping off the main highway to avoid the communist army. Military detachments stopped them twice, but, to their relief, each time it was a Nationalist intelligence company looking for spies in the territory. Each time they were allowed to go on.

Just before dark the ancient walls of Kaifeng came into sight. Missionaries in the capital city welcomed the Hillises into their home. The worn-out children were put to bed, and Dick and Margaret settled comfortably to visit with their hosts, medical missionaries at CIM's hospital compound in Kaifeng.

"Saying good-bye to our Christian brothers and sisters in Loho was very hard," Dick shared with them, his voice weary and sad. "I pray they will be safe and strong in the Lord. In the meantime, we are determined to start our work again—here in Kaifeng. We should be safe behind the city's thick walls."

The compound doctor looked intently at Dick, lowered his eyes, and then said slowly, "Dick, I'm sorry, but the mission authorities have ordered you to proceed to Shanghai as quickly as possible."

Dick could not believe what he was hearing. His face registered the shock and distress that was flooding his mind. Get out? It couldn't be true. Those words were spat in his face once before, by a communist lieutenant. But he never imagined he would hear them from a friend.

Honan had been his home for fourteen years. The work there was his life. It was impossible to think of leaving, never returning to the place that had taught him so much, toughened him into spiritual manhood, made him learn intimately of God's provision and preeminence. He loved the farmers and peasants of that region. He loved the land.

He sat stunned, a film of memories playing through his mind as if in fast motion: the first long years of barrenness, the struggle with the language, the years of harvest—with farmers turned into fishers of men. The experiences had put steel in his soul.

He had watched the idols and ancestral tablets destroyed, had seen the gods of wood burned—he was rich with the memories of God's workings in these people. God *had* worked in the Chinese people—through *him*. It was God's work, he knew. But he had rejoiced in it and lived with no other desire than to continue in that work.

In the years since 1933 he had seen his Chinese brothers crushed by the invading Japanese. He had seen them persecuted by the Communists who set about to destroy their way of life. He had watched the church pass through the purifying flames of suffering. And now he had been ordered to leave. Honan was closed to him. It was over. He must leave the people whose faith had grown strong and vigorous through pain and war, the people who had taught him much about his own faith.

There is no way to measure the grief Dick felt as he and his family boarded the plane that carried them from Kaifeng to Shanghai. There is no way to count the tears that fell in his heart.

"No, God, it can't be!" he cried.

Rebellion shouted, "No, I won't get out!" even as the engines roared and the plane carried him to Shanghai.

When the enemies of Israel prevailed against David, the king, he cried to God, "Put my tears into Thy bottle." As Dick peered through the window of the plane and watched the Honan region disappear from sight, his tears poured into the bottle and mingled with those of a king.

But David, the shepherd-psalmist, also wrote, "Weeping may endure for a night, but joy cometh in the morning."

Dick wiped his tears and opened his eyes to new joys and challenges in the port city of Shanghai, the city that had called to him in his boyhood. And as he did, his optimism returned.

The Communists could never cross the wide Yangtze River, he was sure, so he could begin new work with the Chinese people he loved, although he would have to adjust to Shanghai and the life of a city dweller. It would be different after the quiet, agricultural life of the Honan, but different was just that: not better or worse. He would adapt.

He began teaching at the China Bible Seminary, where he found the students to be eager, quick learners. Their hunger for the Word of God and for every lesson one could share with them helped to heal the wound of being driven out of Honan. The days and months passed peacefully until one Thursday.

The day began routinely with a motorcycle ride out through the crowded Shanghai marketplace to the quieter countryside where the seminary was located. Formal classes were over by noon, but the students and Dick continued their discussions about the Scripture over a lunch of rice, bean sprouts, and fish.

As soon as the last grain of rice was cleaned from his bowl, Dick climbed on his cycle and headed to an important errand in a small village not far away. He was in a hurry and sped over the bumpy roads. But he came to an abrupt halt when he entered the village. There in the marketplace were scores of soldiers, each with a red cloth tied to his revolver.

No one had to tell him the meaning of the red cloth. This was the communist army, knocking at the very doors of Shanghai, a city living in a fool's paradise, believing a mere river could hold back the advance of communist soldiers.

It was only a week before the Communists took over the seminary. Again they heard the command, "Get out!" The city of Shanghai fell with hardly a shot fired, and the missionaries became prisoners in their compound. They could come and go about the city, but could not attend the churches as that would endanger the Chinese Christians.

After months of inactivity, with every movement observed and restricted by the Red soldiers, they received their final orders. Again, "Get out! Get out of China!"

The new government refused to let them leave from the Shanghai harbor. Instead they sent them north to Tientsin.

It was a long and wearying trip, especially hard on the five children and Margaret, who was seven months pregnant. They traveled up to Nanking by train, crossed the Yangtze River by ferry, and then took the train for two days and two nights across China to Tientsin.

When they arrived in the northern port city they were sure the worst was over, but soon discovered that the communist officials were determined to make their exit as difficult as possible. Dick spent two days signing meaningless papers and trying to keep from losing his already frayed temper.

On the third day they were ordered to report to the wharf for inspection at five in the morning. There they stood for hours as the sun rose and heated the day to sweltering temperatures. Margaret held Jennifer, the youngest of the children, and tried to find a way to cool her feverish body. The other children grew tired, hot, hungry, and restless. After seven hours of waiting the first immigration inspectors arrived.

Hours later, in late afternoon, the customs officers opened their bags, and several hours after that they were finally ordered to board a dismal coal scow in the company of two hundred other refugees.

Crowded down in the scow's dark, stale-smelling interior, Dick and Margaret clutched the children tightly. Sounds of crying and confusion filled the darkened space as they waited to begin the next step in their journey.

The destination was an American ship, *General Gordon,* standing at anchor outside the Taku Bar, twelve miles off the coast of China. They had hoped to be on board by nightfall, but the sun was beginning to set before they heard the first sound of the tug's motor.

When they finally moved into the stormy open sea, the low-riding scow began to roll and toss frightfully. Babies and children wailed in fear. Seasickness added to the misery.

They finally reached the *General Gordon* only to find that their long night on the scow was not over. The captain would not let them board. A climb on a narrow ladder up the sides of a swaying ship in the blackness of night was a much too dangerous feat for the inexperienced people waiting to board.

At 4:00 A.M., as the sea calmed and the early dawn brought dim light, the passengers were allowed to make the climb. On the deck friendly American sailors greeted them and, below, hot coffee and warm, clean beds awaited them.

As he drank the hot brew and felt its warmth inside him, Dick began to feel his body relax. For the first time in months his family was safe. For the first time in months he slept without fear.

But safety proved to be a relative term. True, they were safe from the destruction and violence of war; safe from the aggression of the communist enemies. But the dangers were not altogether behind them.

The thirty-one-day voyage was distorted with nightmarish effects. Mealtimes resembled scenes from a prison film. Passengers lined up and food was dumped on naval plates as each one filed past the crewmen.

Men and boys slept in bunks stacked four high. The women slept in a separate section where they tended the younger children. Margaret got little rest because of the crying babies all around her. Her own children were exhausted and uncomfortable.

Many of the refugees were weak already, and the long voyage only served to worsen their condition. The vessel stopped three times for burial at sea.

One constant question plagued Dick's thoughts: Was it all a waste? Each roll of the ocean seemed to rock him with despair and an increasing sense of futility. His mind was weary with defeat. How could he face the future without despair, he wondered.

For fourteen years China had been his only world. Were all those years wasted? Would failure sign its name to the story of fourteen years in the Chinese province of Honan?

The questions were persistent, but so was the answer God gave him. It was as if he could hear God's voice, reassuring him, comforting him, loving him with His words: "Being confident of this very thing, that he which hath begun a good work in you will perform it until the day of Jesus Christ" (Philippians 1:6).

He listened to the Holy Spirit and felt himself grow quiet inside. Hope entered his mind as it became clear to him: the work begun in the lives of the Christian brothers and sisters in China would not die out! God—not the Red army—would be preeminent.

Didn't Jesus face this same issue with His disciples as He prepared them for His leaving? Dick mused. They would indeed bring forth fruit, and that fruit would remain. Nineteen centuries could not diminish the force of the Word, nor the power of the One who spoke it!

The happy news of Jesus Christ had freed the Chinese farmers and peasants from a life bound tightly in superstition and fear. Though their future appeared uncertain, it was now bound tightly in the promises of the one true God, the "Nothing-He-Cannot-Do-One."

As Dick stood on the deck of the *General Gordon,* feeling the spray of wind and ocean across his face, he breathed in the pure sweet smell of it and a fresh wind of confidence girded him. He released his Chinese brothers and sisters to the care of His Father. And with a new sense of determination he handed over to Him his own future and that of his family.

18

Something No One Else Can Do

On May 23, 1950, the *General Gordon* pulled into harbor. America! The land of the free. As Dick watched the West Coast shoreline come into view he thought of how significant those words are: a land free from aggression and turmoil, a land free from fear. It was good to be home after all.

But Dick knew he faced a period of adjustment. It would take time to assuage the heartache he felt at having to leave China. He was now thirty-seven years old, and all the adult years of his life had been lived in the Orient. He was practically Chinese himself now.

He had been hardly more than a boy when he arrived in China at twenty years old. For years he had lived the Chinese way of life. He had adopted their attitudes, thought in their thought patterns, eaten their food, read their books, written their characters. China was his home. Even during the months of furlough in the States he had felt displaced, anxious to get back to his people, his land, his work.

I'll be a stranger here, he thought as he looked out at the coastline coming closer with each moment. Then he gave himself a mental shake. Of course it would take time, but he would settle into a new life. This was a day for thinking of the future, not brooding over the past.

A plan had begun to form in Dick's mind since the early days of the voyage home. He had decided to become a missions and church history professor at some Christian school, just as he had done during a furlough years back. The blueprint was sketched in his mind, a blueprint for his future.

But the helpmate the Lord had given him gently probed him, urging him to be sure of what God wanted. "Dick, are you sure this is what God has for us?" Her questions made him pause to wonder if maybe he was trying to help God work out the details of his life.

But a teaching profession seemed a good choice. He was the father of five children, and another one was due in a few short weeks. A teaching profession was a good, secure career for a family. So it was decided. He settled on that goal and prayed for God's blessing.

But God refused to stamp "Approved" on that plan for the future. Instead, He placed another blueprint before Dick and asked not for Dick's approval, but for his joyful acceptance.

It happened that summer of 1950, just six weeks after the Hillises returned home. Dick settled his young family in Yakima, Washington, just ten days after Margaret gave birth to Brian. Then, in July, Dick was invited to attend a one-week conference for a young missionary organization called Youth For Christ. He traveled to a Bible Conference in Warsaw, Indiana, called Winona Lake.

There Dick's war-damaged spirits were soothed in the peaceful atmosphere of the lake-side conference grounds. He basked in the fellowship of old friendships and made new friends as well.

Each night he joined hundreds of conference visitors and campers as they made their way to the huge, open air auditorium. There in the Billy Sunday Tabernacle they sang the great old hymns and listened to the enthusiastic reports of the young missionary endeavor. Already the country's youth had been thrilled by such young men as Billy Graham and Torrey Johnson, men who had risen to leadership through YFC. It was exciting to learn of the Spirit's work elsewhere in the world while he and Margaret had been busy in China.

Though the Indiana evenings were hot, muggy, and noisy with the drone of attacking mosquitos, Dick gave no thought to discomfort. This was just what he needed. He raised his voice with the others and sang with great emotion. The familiar songs rolled about in the tabernacle and resounded with a special beauty. He could already feel the healing effects on his spirit. He could feel the return of peace to his mind and body.

But it was a short-lived peace. In the middle of the week, Bob Pierce, a speaker on the program for the YFC conference, dropped a bomb on Dick that destroyed all his well-drawn plans and goals.

"A cry for help has come to the Christians of America," he announced to the congregation during the evening meeting. "Madame Chiang kai-Shek, wife of the president of Free China, has asked for someone to come out to Taiwan and preach to the soldiers who have escaped from the Communists.

Thousands have fled the mainland and have taken refuge on the island since the communist invasion. They have left their homes and many of their family members behind. They are defeated and discouraged.

"Madame Chiang has already begun a women's prayer group in Taiwan. It is growing in size and fame. Now she wants desperately for the soldiers who have followed her husband to freedom in Taiwan to learn of the saving grace of Jesus Christ," he continued. "She is pleading for someone to *please* come and preach the gospel to the thousands who need the message of hope."

Dick felt his chest tighten. He closed his eyes and sat very still in his seat.

Bob Pierce went on. "There is a man here tonight who could go and do this very thing," he said. "He has just returned from China and has himself experienced the pain of being ousted from the land he loves. Dick Hillis, I am going to ask you to come forward. Let us pray for you, that God would direct you into this new ministry, if that is His will."

Dick's legs were wooden as he stood. He tried to draw a full breath and steady his heartbeats. His reluctant feet left a trail in the sawdust floor of the Billy Sunday tabernacle as he walked up to the platform. With a sense of unreality he knelt.

A group of young men gathered around him. Among them was the budding evangelist Billy Graham. Together they put their hands on his head and prayed for God's blessing upon him and this new work.

Dick's head was bowed, but his spirit was rising in rebellion. "Lord, I'm not going to Taiwan. I just escaped from the Communists. I have been caught once and I am not going to get caught a second time. That island is only a hundred miles from mainland China , and it is doomed to fall. Lord, how can I explain it to these men? They cannot understand, but You do, Lord. You have something for me to do *here,* in America, Lord. I'm going to teach. It has already been decided. My plans are made. Please understand, Lord—"

The evening service ended a short while later. Dick made his way through the tree-shadowed night, hardly seeing anyone or anything in his path. All he wanted was the privacy of his tiny room. He closed the door and let his body sag onto the small bed against the wall. He knew with a sense of sadness that his peaceful retreat was over. Unwittingly, he had entered another battle zone.

Dick's struggle stretched throughout the long hours of the night. He prayed, argued, and wrestled with God. The prayers of the men on that platform had made an enormous emotional impact on him. He could not dismiss lightly the need that had been laid on him, nor the dread he felt at the thought of answering that need.

His feelings were in a state of flux. Like a pendulum his emotions swung between fear for himself and concern for a people he loved. Half a million

Chinese soldiers were lost. They had lost their homes, their land, their loved ones, everything that was dear to them. Their ancient civilization, over thousands of years old, lay ransacked. They had no past. Defeated and discouraged, they could see no future, no reason to live. They were demoralized and depressed. Some had committed suicide. Others wanted to but lacked the courage.

The hours of that night were a lonely, dark passage as Dick walked the floor and prayed. Surely there was merit to the idea of teaching missions here in America, he kept telling himself—and God.

What God told Dick that night had merit too, however.

The Spirit reminded him of an ethical imperative God had taught him many years ago. "Never do what someone else can do if you can do something no one else can do."

This thought so gripped him it was impossible to even think of sleep. He knew there were hundreds of men qualified to teach missions and church history at Christian schools in America. But how many men were there who knew the Chinese culture and could preach in Mandarin to the defeated Chinese soldiers who had escaped to the island of Taiwan?

When he closed his eyes to seek sleep, the picture of a tall man and a short, stocky woman filled his mind. The Dicksons were a missionary couple he had met on the boat as he and his family returned to China in 1946 after their furlough. Lillian Dickson played her accordion for the children and led them in Bible classes during the long days of the voyage. Jim and Dick spent many hours talking about the work in their fields. The ship docked first in Shanghai, and as the Hillises departed, Jim called to Dick and said, "If you ever have to leave mainland China, come to Taiwan. The need is great."

Now the need was even greater. Dick knew he could not ignore the plea from Madame Chiang kai-Shek. But he also knew he could not ignore his reponsibilities to his own family, to Margaret and the children.

"Lord," he prayed, "I have to know for certain that this is a call from You. And I must know that my family will be cared for somehow, if I am to undertake this new work."

Like Gideon, he demanded proof—several proofs.

"I must have at least three hundred dollars a month support for Margaret and the children while I am gone, Father," he prayed. "And I must have one hundred dollars a month support for my own needs so that I don't have to sponge off any other missionaries on the island. And Lord, I know that Jesus most often sent men out in twos to do His work. So I am asking you to give me a partner, someone to go with me. And this will confirm in my mind that You do want me to go.

"And there is something else. I want to be able to give a free gospel of

John in the Chinese language to everyone I preach to."

That would mean securing several thousand Chinese texts, from where and from whom he was unsure. Last of all, he asked the Lord to give him strong evidence from Madame Chiang that the door to Taiwan really was open, that he would have ready access to the troops.

Then, as if in an afterthought, Dick added one more stipulation. "Lord, I will only go for three months, and I must have a round-trip ticket in my hand before leaving.

"If You accomplish all this, Lord, then I will know that this assignment is from You. I will know You want me in Taiwan."

The conference continued, and each day Dick placed his conditions before the Lord. He wondered, *Will God meet my conditions?* Internally, his struggle intensified.

One night, after a lengthy, enthusiastic service in the Billy Sunday tabernacle, as Dick was getting ready for bed, there was a knock on his door.

"Come in," Dick called.

A young man in his early twenties stepped into the room. "My name is Ells Culver," he said. "I heard the call for someone to go to Taiwan. The next day I heard that you were considering the idea but felt you shouldn't go alone."

Dick studied the young man. "Yes, that's right," he answered.

"Well," continued Ells, "I haven't been able to sleep since then."

Dick grinned knowingly, nodded his head, and waited for the young man to continue.

"I think God wants me to go with you."

Dick wasn't certain how to respond. Was this God's first step in fulfilling the conditions Dick had laid down?

Ells was a young pastor and the son of missionary parents. He had been married only a short time and had a baby girl.

"You know you will have to raise your own support and travel expenses," Dick told him, his eyes never leaving the young man's face. "It will mean leaving your wife and daughter for three months. You'd better go back and pray about it more, Ells."

At the end of the week, Ells stood in front of Dick and gave him his word that he would go to Taiwan with him. Dick found it hard to summon a thankful spirit, even though the news was an answer to prayer. He packed and left Winona Lake with a sense of heaviness in his spirit.

When he arrived back in Washington, Dick shared with Margaret the burden of Taiwan that had been laid upon him the past week. Back and forth they considered the interminable questions.

"Where will the children and I live?" Margaret asked. "*How* will we live?"

Dick told her of the conditions he had laid before the Lord and together they prayed for each one: the financial support, the freedom to preach once there in Taiwan, the gospels of John to give to the soldiers, a place for his family to stay.

Even in the face of the obstacles Dick could not escape the urgency of God's will. As the days passed he could not deny the power of God to provide and direct. Within forty-five days he heard again from Ells: he had all the support he needed. Two weeks later all of Dick's support was accounted for. And thrown in was a bonus: Dick would have not one, but *two* men to accompany him. The third member of the team was to be Uri Chandler, a young missionary from the Oriental Missionary Society.

Under the banner of Youth For Christ, the three men set their faces for Taiwan. The plan was a three-month preaching tour, then return home to their families, the work done, the subject closed.

With the plans settled, Dick moved his family to a home in Glendale, California, provided by the Church of the Open Door. Then he began making preparations for his departure, once again, to the Orient.

19

Assignment: Republic of China—Taiwan

In the sixteenth century, Portuguese explorers named Taiwan *Formosa,* meaning beautiful. Coastal plains sweep upward to mountain ranges of over 10,000 feet. Beige beaches blend into the variegated greens of rice fields and lowland meadows, then deepen into the dense, dark shades of the rain forests. From his window seat on the plane, Dick saw the same beauty that had amazed the early sailors.

Glistening off the western coast of the island lay the one-hundred-mile stretch of sea called the Formosa Strait, its narrow expanse the only distance between Mao's feared aggressors and the tentative safety of Taiwan.

It was October 24, 1950. Dick watched as the plane leveled and approached the runway below. As the ground came closer and closer Dick struggled to control the apprehension he felt. The words of the fierce young lieutenant rang in his ears.

"I will die to carry Communism one mile farther!"

His dedication to the revolution had indeed cost him his life. His commitment had caused Dick to examine the degree of his own commitment. How far was he willing to go for the cause of Jesus Christ? At what cost would he carry the gospel of Jesus Christ "one mile farther?"

Dick thought of the thousands of miles that separated him from his wife and children. At that lonely moment, half a world away from his family, the cost seemed very great. He prayed the three-month assignment would pass quickly so he could return to the States and begin the new life he had planned. He was anxious to be as far away as possible from the communist forces that had more than once threatened his life and his family and had ultimately robbed him of the ministry he loved among the people of Honan.

The plane touched down on the narrow airstrip, and Dick's eyes scanned the area. As he caught sight of the familiar face of a tall, lean man, excitement and joy replaced his earlier emotions. Jim Dickson stood waiting to welcome him to the island country that would be his home for the next three months.

It had been several years since that shipboard conversation between the two men. But Dick had not forgotten that of all the foreigners living on the island, Jim and his wife Lillian knew Taiwan and its people better than any.

When Jim and Lillian arrived in Taiwan in 1927, under the banner of the Presbyterian Church of Canada, they were appalled by the disease and squalor and corruption that greeted them. They were even more appalled by the fact that such conditions were taken for granted.

Former headhunter tribes still lived in the mountains. Large numbers of little girls were sold into prostitution. Though leprosy clinics existed, the conditions were so deplorable and the patients so miserable that three suicides per week were recorded.

Lillian saw the sorrow and desperation as a "sea of suffering" and said of it, "I'm going to take out my bucketful." And she proceeded to make changes wherever she went.

Her small stature was a stark contrast to the size of her ideas. She was responsible for the establishment of one hundred churches and one hundred kindergartens which served over 5,000 children. She worked to get schools for aboriginal boys, where they could learn farming skills, and classes for girls to learn homemaking.

At her insistence, the leprosy clinics were whitewashed, their linens burned, and clean ones brought in. Music was piped into the wards, and family visiting hours were established.

Lillian's special love for children made her welcome wherever she went. She was seldom seen without her accordion. Called the "Pied Piper for Christ," she trekked into the mountains with Jim to sing and play for the children while he preached and taught the Bible to adults.

The death rate of infants and mothers on Taiwan prompted her to seek help to build maternity wards. Though finances were always a struggle, she said more than once, "We work on a shoestring, but it is God's shoestring."

Jim's ideas were often pushed through to fruition by the little woman whose size was no obstacle to her ambition for God. Her unmatched energy and unquestioning faith was a continual challenge to the Canadian mission that sent them to the island country.

Since their arrival on Taiwan, they had survived the Japanese occupation, spoke Taiwanese clearly, knew people in government, and knew the condition of the church on the island. They had the answer to any question that could arise. As veteran missionaries, their support was essential to the work planned for the three young men from America. It was into the Dickson home that the three were welcomed that fall day in 1950. The headquarters for their work on the island was to be that home, and their hosts and mentors for the duration of their stay were the indomitable team of Jim and Lillian Dickson.

The trio barely had time to unpack before their work began—there was to be no time wasted. The day after their arrival they were summoned by Madame Chiang's secretary.

"Your ministry among the soldiers is of the highest priority," they were told. "We will do everything possible to assist you."

Soon after the meeting, Dick left for a city to the south where thousands of Chinese versions of the gospel of John were waiting for him. The gospels, printed in Hong Kong and authorized by Madame Chiang, passed through the customs system with ease. Dick recalled the many struggles encountered with Chinese customs officials in the past, and he breathed a prayer of thanks as the books were passed through without question or hesitation.

Back in the Dickson home, the men prepared their schedule for the ministry to the soldiers. On the night before they were to begin preaching sleep was impossible. Anticipation and fear mingled inside them. They knew intuitively that they were embarking on something unique, yet they had no way of knowing that the days of ministry ahead of them would be the most exciting they would ever experience.

The next morning was greeted with a mixture of surprise and uncertainty. A weapons carrier arrived at the front door of the Dicksons' home to take them to barracks to preach. The taxi service, arranged by Madame Chiang's prayer group, presented a ferocious appearance until the men understood the kindness behind its arrival.

At the barracks Dick and his co-workers found the commandant ready and waiting with tea for them. Every day followed the format begun that first day: the unusual taxi-cab ride, tea with each commandant, and then a walk to the parade grounds where the soldiers were lined up and waiting for the preaching to begin.

That first day, as the three looked out over the sea of khaki-clad men, quiet and attentive, waiting to be fed the life-giving words of Jesus, a sense of awe came over them. Thousands of soldiers were commanded to be still and listen to the preaching of the word of God. And they waited patiently for the preaching to begin.

Dick was the first of the three missionaries to begin.

"How many of you have ever heard of Jesus Christ before?" he asked. Some raised their hands and told of learning from missionaries on the mainland.

Then he asked, "How many of you have never heard of Jesus Christ?" He was astounded as more than one-third of the soldiers raised hands. He breathed a silent prayer for God's Spirit to move and work among the men, then he read them a letter from their leader, General Chiang kai-Shek:

> I am very pleased to exhort people to read the Bible because it is the voice of the Holy Spirit. Enlarging the righteousness and compassion of God toward the men of the world. And the Savior, Jesus Christ. His love can cover our sins, and all those who believe in Jesus will get eternal life.
>
> President Chiang

Then the gospels of John were passed out to all the men so they could follow along in the Bible as they listened to the preaching.

Each day, in every military post, the pattern was the same. Each meeting was begun with the questions, and always the response was the same. A third of the soldiers had never heard of Jesus.

"The men seemingly never get tired or restless listening to the Word," Dick wrote home. "After the meeting is over I give them a little exhortation from John 14, on the return of Christ to the world. Then we leave with these words, 'If the Lord tarries, and we don't see you anymore on the island of Formosa, we'll see you over on the mainland!' The men break out into a great ovation, for they are looking forward to seeing their loved ones on the mainland."

Dick, Uri, and Ells were overwhelmed by the responsiveness of the soldiers. On the bottom of one of the decision slips, one soldier wrote, "Won't you hurry back and tell us more about Jesus Christ?"

Their eyes filled with tears many times as they finished preaching and watched the men march from the gathering, waving and smiling. "There is something that tears at our hearts," Dick wrote Margaret, "seeing these men without sham and bigotry, but polite and sincere."

One after another the soldiers responded to the new life offered in Jesus Christ. Entire families came to know the salvation God provided through Jesus. And large numbers of them grew hungry to know more, to know God better.

The most logical way to help teach the new believers in their faith was to integrate them into the churches on Taiwan. But these churches were helpless to meet the spiritual needs of the displaced mainland Chinese. They spoke different languages. The islanders spoke Taiwanese while the mainland Chinese understood only Mandarin.

It was a serious dilemma. Without a means to teach these new believers, their faith might founder. Something must be done to strengthen them and encourage them in their new life with Christ.

Dick, Uri, and Ells spent hours in prayer and discussion, trying to determine the best way to disciple the many who had indicated their interest in Jesus Christ as Savior. More than 5,000 men and their families had decided to follow Jesus. What were three men among so many?

One possible solution was a correspondence course. Years earlier, when Dick was in Shanghai under the China Inland Mission, the Navigators Bible correspondence course had been translated into Chinese. That seemed the perfect solution for discipling such a multitude.

So in November, just a month after "Assignment: Taiwan" had been initiated, the Navigators' course was added to the missionary scheme. In response to a request, Dawson Trotman, president of the Navigators, sent two Navigators to join the team and help with the additional task of administrating the course.

Again, the Dicksons' home was the central location. The men corrected the correspondence lessons on the dining room table. Together the handful of missionaries worked out a plan for follow-up on the thousands of Chinese who were beginning the Christian life.

Jim and Lillian, while being the hub of the American team's activities, still had their own missionary responsibilities. They included a grueling schedule of trips to the non-Chinese groups beyond the barracks of the army bases on Taiwan, beyond the city dwellers, into the mountain peoples of the rain forests.

Dick was amazed at the energy and enthusiasm he saw in Jim. In spite of his own demanding routine, he made time to discuss with Dick the needs of the people on the island. The discussions stretched to many hours as they talked about the work of the local churches.

"There are about 30,000 believers on the island," Jim shared with Dick during one late-night discussion. "The church is of Canadian and English Presbyterian background and is basically clergy controlled.

"The clergy," he went on, "does all the work in the church. The believers provide them with only a meager salary. They have no concept of participating in the work, witnessing themselves."

Dick's interest was captured. He leaned forward and found himself listening intently as Jim went on.

"What we need is to train the laity to share the gospel with the rest of the islanders. That is the only way the twelve million people of Taiwan can ever be reached."

Despite the thrill of the challenge, Dick felt that familiar heaviness of a few trying to reach many. He remembered his long, weary, sleepless nights in the Honan province of China, when he wrestled with the problem of how to bring the gospel to the 1.5 million people of that region. God's answer then was to enlist the energies of the believers—to motivate them, train them, and to mobilize them. Farmers of the land had been turned into fishers of men.

Could the city businessmen, the housewives, the bus drivers on this island also be turned into fishermen? Could the lowland rice farmers and aboriginal tribesmen? Dick's concern for the rest of the island of Taiwan, not just the military, Mandarin-speaking population, but the whole, was stimulated.

A few days later, when the barracks were closed for military exercises, Dick accompanied Jim on a preaching trip into the mountains.

As he trekked through the dense jungles of the island he saw hundreds of people, other ethnic tribes, non-Chinese, who would perish without the happy news. For most of his life his great burden had been for the Chinese. He had prayed for them, ministered to them, led them, and loved them. But now, seeing the faces of other peoples who had never heard of God's love, his vision began to swell to include more than just the Chinese. He began to feel concern for those beyond the bamboo and barracks.

Dick was soon spending all his spare time trudging through the forests with Jim. The first time he preached and gave his testimony was like the first time so many years ago in China. It had been a long time since he had felt the mixture of fear and exhilaration he had known so long ago as a novice missionary. But there among the aboriginal tribes, speaking through an interpreter, he felt like a beginner again.

He spoke slowly and listened to the interpreter repeat the gospel in a language that, to him, sounded garbled and nonsensical. Then he watched with awe as eager men and women accepted the truth. Jim's desire to see the whole of Taiwan evangelized became Dick's desire as well: twelve million islanders for Jesus Christ.

"Every heart without Christ is a mission field, every heart with Christ is a missionary." Dick was excited. "Lord," he prayed, "the same principle could be applied here in Taiwan as it was in Shenkiu. No land can be fully reached for Jesus unless every believer becomes a witness. We must see laymen trained!"

Now the work in Taiwan took on new meaning and importance for Dick. A well-defined goal began to form in his mind: to assist the local believers in reaching their nation for Christ.

Jim had said there were already 30,000 Christians on Taiwan. *This is a great pool of manpower,* Dick thought. *But they need tools, visual aids, implements for teaching and preaching.*

The enormity of the task of evangelizing an entire nation seemed overwhelming. Yet how could he consider a lesser goal? Always, as he was preaching in the barracks or climbing to the mountain villages, he was thinking and praying about ways to implement the plan that would reach all of Taiwan.

The three months passed quickly, as he had prayed they would, and as the assignment neared its end, Jim and Dick sat down to spend another evening discussing the work and the island's needs.

"Dick, you must come back. Taiwan needs you. I doubt that the Presbyterian mission board would accept you—your group is such a denominational mix. But perhaps you could begin a new mission. Think about it."

Come back? Lately Dick *had* been wondering how he could leave it all behind without another thought at the end of the three months. But form a mission? That thought had never occurred to him. Yet he had to admit the idea had merit. And the idea of going home to a teaching career had, over the last few weeks, grown less and less appealing. Maybe it could be done. Maybe this was God's plan: to start a new mission organization that would be the means of reaching the island nation of Taiwan for Jesus Christ!

The three months came to an end and Dick and his co-workers packed up to go home. Uri and Ells flew straight home to their families, but Dick scheduled a stop in Washington, D.C., to meet with the executive director of the Evangelical Foreign Mission Association. Dr. Clyde Taylor and his assistant spent several hours listening and discussing with Dick the formation of a mission.

"It would be primarily involved in edifying the church through the training of its laity, so that the entire nation could be reached. It would be a service mission," Dick explained.

The excitement and enthusiasm he felt for this idea was contagious. He shared with the men the needs of the country and the great harvest he had already witnessed. They talked about the ideas Dick and Jim Dickson had discussed, and he found them encouraging and supportive. But he had no idea what was necessary for the creation of a mission.

"The paperwork is simple enough," Dr. Taylor said. "And then you pay the incorporation fee of ten dollars."

"But I don't have it!" Dick blurted. "I'm not even sure how I'm going to come up with taxi fare to get from here to the airport so I can fly the rest of the way home!"

"I've got a few dollars in my pocket," Dr. Taylor volunteered.

"And I can shell out a couple," offered his assistant.

And between the two men the ten-dollar incorporation fee was paid.

Dick was exuberant but exhausted. The flight from Taiwan to Washington, D.C., and the day of meetings had drained the last of his energy.

"Dick, I'm taking you home with me," Clyde told him. "You need a meal and a night's rest before you start for California."

The next morning Dr. Taylor drove him to the airport and put him on a plane for Los Angeles. Dick arrived home with no money in his pockets but filled with news to share with Margaret.

"We're going back to Taiwan. But this time you and the children are going with me," he told Margaret and the children. "And it's not just for three months."

20

White Fields

"March, 1951," Dick wrote in his journal. "Leaving soon for the harvest in Formosa. I am keenly aware of the cost of leaving. It seems there is no crown without a cross, no following without a fight, no birth without suffering, no harvest without sacrifice."

Dick knew he faced months of grueling work. Homes had to be found on the island for the families he and his companions were taking back with them. Financial support had to be secured. And there was the ever-present knowledge that he was again plunging his family into a foreign culture just one hundred miles from the land that had only months earlier forced them out at gunpoint. Yet he could see past the difficulties to the joy that lay beyond.

In China a small band of Shenkiu farmers had gone out to their own people to preach. Farmers had become fishermen, and the catch had been mighty! It was Jesus' own example of evangelism and discipling, and Dick would not tamper with the method that He had implemented among His disciples. The plan on Taiwan was the same: train islanders to minister to their own people.

Anticipation encouraged him through the hectic summer of 1951. He spent some time at home with his family, then went back to Taiwan to help Ells get settled and started with the correspondence course. Village evangelism got underway, and helpers for the military work were recruited.

Then it was back again to Los Angeles where Dick and Margaret prepared for the trip to Taiwan. Though the preparations were tedious, Margaret was happier than she had been in months.

The separation she and the children had endured during "Assignment: Taiwan" had been grueling. During her years in China she had had the help of Chinese workers as she cared for the younger children of the family, and the older children had attended boarding school. Dick's presence had been dependable. But in Los Angeles she was alone in a two-bedroom cottage with six children, one a newborn. Suddenly she had to marshal all her energies to cope and remain steady and cheerful.

On Dick's return she learned of the move that was ahead and the challenge of deputation work that must come first. Even those things did not seem so overwhelming when she reminded herself that they would be together again, living as a family on the island of Taiwan.

Dick began a schedule of speaking engagements, church conferences, and radio broadcasts. Each engagement gave needed exposure to the fledgling mission organization and raised interest as well as prayer and financial support. Dinners, meetings with such evangelists as Billy Graham and his team, helped the young mission gain visibility. The months were filled with traveling, speaking, and showing films that depicted the work in Taiwan.

Meanwhile, the workers already in Taiwan were busy. Constant reports flowed in to Dick of the miracles occurring on the island. A summer visitor wrote to say, "I have seen a greater harvest in Formosa in these few weeks than in seventeen years of ministry at home."

And another, "That one soldiers' meeting accomplished more than all my summer's conference work."

One worker who joined the staff of the young mission wrote, "This last month we distributed 60,000 gospels of John, ministered to 100,000 people, and saw 7,000 indicate their desire to know Christ."

That summer was the beginning of intensive work among the tribespeople. The first church leaders' conference was held and over seventy pastors attended.

More than 10,000 decisions for Christ were made on the island of Taiwan that summer. As reports of the excitement continued to come in, Dick grew more anxious to get back. But first it was necessary to establish an administrative staff for the mission.

With money that came in during the deputation work they were able to buy property in Los Angeles and put together a small staff. Dick's father served as temporary Home Director. Soon after, Norman Cummings, formerly of Youth For Christ, took over, and the first board of directors was assembled.

The mission began to function, dealing with budgets and personnel and supplying the field representatives with prayer support daily.

Finally, in November 1951, after months of preparation, Dick and Margaret and their six children boarded the *Jean Lafitte* and set sail for the Orient. The miserable voyage was plagued by storms and seasickness. As the ship tossed about, dishes crashed in the poorly supplied galley. Supplies of food and milk ran out long before they arrived at their destination in Japan.

The exhausted family left the ship and boarded a plane for the last leg of the journey. On December 12, they landed on Taiwan.

Jim and Lillian Dickson had prayed for years that God would send them 200 missionaries to help with the island work. "But we forgot to stipulate Presbyterian!" they quipped.

What they received was a harmonious blend of many already existing organizations cooperating with one vision, one purpose: To motivate, train, and mobilize the believers on Taiwan to evangelize their own nation.

Navigators supplied the correspondence course in use, as well as the men to administer it. The Oriental Missionary Society and Youth For Christ blended manpower and efforts. People such as Mrs. Billy Sunday and Mrs. Charles Cowman, whose husband founded the Oriental Missionary Society, became involved financially.

It was a unique combination of energies and efforts: the supernatural power of the Holy Spirit, the willing minds and bodies of the missionaries, the political power of the islands directed by General and Madame Chiang kai-Shek.

The impact of the mission was seen everywhere on the island. But its name was not so easily known. For a time the work was done under the name of Gospel Outreach. Stationery with the initials "G. O." was ordered, but it was never used. Then the name "Formosa Gospel Crusades" began to erupt in conversation and correspondence but was never official. That name soon evolved into Orient Crusades.

Although the name changed as the mission developed, the simple purpose for the mission's existence never varied.

The small country bustled with activities: citywide crusades, prayer meetings, educational and language ministries, all conducted by Baptists, Lutherans, Methodists, Christian and Missionary Alliance, and others. The band of disciplers never had to look for ministry opportunities. The need was always present.

Also present and busy on the island were the Jehovah's Witnesses. Their message nearly cost the Orient Crusades workers the privilege of preaching on the military bases. "If you want to be true Christians you must lay down your weapons" was the pacifist message of the Jehovah's Witnesses.

Immediately the Ministry of National Defense ruled that no more preaching would be allowed on any military base.

The decree sent Dick and the Orient Crusades fellowship to their knees to pray. And Dick went to speak to Madame Chiang kai-Shek. If anyone could revoke this command, she could. With her intervention, under the direction of the Holy Spirit, the Ministry of Defense agreed to print special passports that enabled Dick and his team to continue preaching to the military.

Elsewhere on the island, the ministry of the mission proceeded undaunted. In January 1952 Dick wrote to the headquarters in Los Angeles: "We opened work under the new mission with only a handful of workers. We now have thirteen Chinese workers, twenty-seven aboriginal preachers in the hills, and eight American workers. Over 65,000 have made decisions of one kind or another. One and a half million gospels have been distributed. And 101,000 Bible studies have been sent out."

Later that year, Dick and a team of preachers ventured onto the island of Quemoy. Fear clutched Dick again as he led the team onto the heavily fortified Nationalist outpost in the Formosa Strait. Quemoy was often bombarded by the communist forces on the mainland, and the day they arrived, the Communists tossed fifty shells across the strait at the defenders. Each exploding bomb reminded the team of the imperative to preach the life-giving message of Jesus Christ. For twelve days the team preached to the Nationalist soldiers and saw 13,000 indicate their desire to commit themselves to Jesus Christ.

Ells preached in Quemoy's prison, where eight men became believers in Jesus. The inmates, hungry to learn more, began a Bible study together. Months after the preaching visit, word came back to the mission that the men were still gathering together every day to study the Bible and pray.

One significant victory of that first year was the salvation of the most important Bunnan chieftan on the island of Taiwan. "He is going around the area telling his tribe about the Savior! This could mean the whole Bunnan tribe turning to Christ. Pray for them," Dick wrote home. "Already there are three Bunnan churches and fifteen meeting places. God is at work!"

God *was* at work—through the energies of men who had caught the vision of evangelism. And Taiwan was not enough for them. Their eyes began to rove beyond the island's watery boundaries.

In April 1952, Ells went to the Pescadore Islands to preach to the population of 130,000. After several days of ministry, he wired, "Revival stirring in the islands. Most of these people are fishermen. They are exceedingly superstitious. Forty percent of their income is given to idolatry. Two high priests have believed. Jesus once did much for fishermen. He can do it again."

In a five-day meeting in Magong, the capital of the Pescadores, the team saw over 250 decisions for Jesus Christ. Church members began gathering every morning before daylight for an hour of prayer. Eighty-three families turned to Jesus.

On a routine business trip for the mission, Dick's plane landed on Okinawa to refuel. As Dick looked out the window of the plane, he viewed the terrible devastation of that tiny island that had been the scene of the climax of World War II.

His heart ached as he saw the suffering of the people and the rubble of their once beautiful island home. "There is a great need there," he shared with his team when he returned home. "We must help the people there."

The team was quick to agree, so Orient Crusades continued their march onward and moved into Okinawa. Their goal: to help rebuild the sixteen churches that had been destroyed in the war and to encourage the believers that remained.

Navigators joined hands to work with Orient Crusades' team on Okinawa. They went out among the native tribes and villagers, as well as United States servicemen stationed on the island's huge military base. Thousands responded to the invitation to receive God's gift of Jesus Christ. Servicemen, Japanese islanders, and tribal villagers all stood in the same place of submission before the conviction of the Holy Spirit.

The team on Okinawa determined to reach every village in the Ryukyu Chain, the group of islands of which Okinawa is a part. It was a reasonable goal for men whose power and energy poured from God. And within a short time every village in the chain did hear the gospel of Jesus Christ.

In a unique way, Orient Crusades was witness to, and participant in, God's preservation of the spiritual harvest in those Asian islands of the Formosa Strait. God used the organization to protect the fruit from those who would have destroyed it or snatched it away. The government of Taiwan asked Orient Crusades, as one of the first American organizations in the Formosan territories, to act as "guarantor" for any other Christian groups that might seek entry into the islands.

If the group seeking entry was known to be evangelical, the mission invited them in and agreed to act as guarantor for them. If not, they simply did not respond to the Ministry of Foreign Affairs' letter about them. The group or association was then denied a visa.

The men of Orient Crusades never tired of discovering new methods of evangelism, new ways of teaching and discipling. They were always on the lookout for innovative ideas that would present Jesus Christ to men. One afternoon the idea of sports evangelism was born, bouncing into an already full and active family of ministries.

Dick and Ells, standing on a busy intersection in Taipei one day, saw a crowd of eight thousand people waiting to get into a sports activity in the former military sports arena. Wherever they saw people, Dick and his teammates saw opportunities to witness.

"Could we get a chance to preach the gospel if we had a Christian basketball team?" they asked each other.

The first step was to get the backing of the first family. Dick made an appointment to discuss the idea with Madame Chiang. She responded with enthusiasm. "If you can find the players we will sponsor the team and get them into the country," she promised.

It was Ells's idea to contact Don Odle. Don was the coach at Taylor University at that time and had led his team to championship status.

Heedless of the fact that it was 3:00 A.M. in Indiana, Dick placed a call to Don.

"It's Dick Hillis here. I'm calling from Taiwan," Dick said through the static of the telephone wires. "I'd like you to bring your team to Taiwan."

"Play basketball in Taiwan?" Don asked.

"And preach," Dick added. "We want a team of Christian basketball players—a great team—to give three months of ministry up and down the island, playing the finest teams and holding basketball clinics. At the half-time of each game they will preach, give testimonies, and have a program."

And so they came. And with them came Bud Shaeffer, an All-American player from Wheaton College. The publicity about this project was kept to a minimum; in fact, very little was said except to advertise the games in Taiwan.

"I'm not sure it's going to work," Dick admitted, "but we're going to try it and see."

By the summer's end Dick had put away his doubts about sports evangelism. The team had played 87 games, won 86, and had preached to over 300,000 people.

A young girl, Jenny Yu, was a spectator at one of the many games played since that pivotal summer of 1952. An ardent Buddhist, she would never have considered attending any evangelical church. But she went to a basketball game.

Jenny's class at school had been given five tickets—not nearly enough for all the students in the class. So a lottery was held to pick the children who would be able to go. Jenny's name was one of the five drawn. She and her four friends went to the game and heard the name of Jesus Christ proclaimed as the Savior of the world.

To Jenny, the gospel was truly "good news!" It spoke of a way to have peace with God. It spoke of One who loved her and offered her salvation from her sins and a life of joy. Jesus Christ was offered to her—He would become her friend and her Savior if she would accept Him.

For a long time Jenny had wondered why she should worship the small wooden idols she saw made with men's hands and sold in the back-street shops of her town. She had always dreaded the family trips to the temple where her father brought the ritual offerings. The huge image of Buddha cast eerie shadows around the dark temple. He loomed large and ugly to her eyes, unheeding of the gifts they brought, offering nothing in return.

The practice of worshiping her ancestors was just as perplexing to Jenny. They too, were not alive, and seemed to have no power to help her or give her joy and peace.

But this good news said that the universe had a personal creator, who had been incarnated to reconcile a wayward people to Himself, and would come again for His own. Here was a promise of joy and peace, something she wanted. It spoke of heaven too. Her religion told of heaven as well, but it taught that she must do enough good to merit it. She was always troubled about how much good was "enough." And often she wondered what there was about heaven that she should want to go there.

She was intrigued by the message she heard that night at the basketball game. She was interested in this Jesus. He was Someone who could provide her with the way to enter heaven, and His own presence there made heaven desirable!

The Bible correspondence course was offered after the gospel message was preached. Jenny and her four friends signed up. Not long after that night at the game the five youngsters began attending a Bible study. After a few weeks, Jenny was the only one of the five whose interest remained. She studied and listened week after week. Finally, at home alone one night, she asked Jesus Christ to become her Savior.

As she grew older and matured in her faith, a goal began to form in her mind. She wanted to join the staff of the organization that had first pointed her to Jesus Christ. As soon as she had worked and saved enough money to pay for her airfare, she left her home in Taiwan and joined the headquarters of Orient Crusades in Los Angeles.

Jenny Yu's story is only one of the many thousands that could be told of those who, while attending basketball games, learned of life's greatest prize, God's love in the person of Jesus Christ.

21

The Birth of Overseas Crusades

"Dick, the Philippines needs you. The country is ripe for the kind of work you are doing. Won't you consider sending a team there, too?"

The request came from Billy Graham. He had just finished a tour of the Philippines and was making a stop in Taiwan. His question was a challenge to the little mission that had never visualized itself reaching beyond the Formosa Strait.

Dick's vision began to expand again, this time to view the whole Orient. When an official invitation came from the Philippine church asking the Orient Crusades into their country, his answer was yes. The team entered the country with the purpose of teaching the believers on the islands how to evangelize their own people, how to disciple their own nation. "Every Christian a witness" was the group's motto.

Within a short time another opportunity was presented to the young mission. The church in Vietnam issued an urgent request. "Will you please come to Tourane [now Da Nang] for a national pastors' conference and explain what you believe to be the proper methodology of evangelism and discipling?"

Dick studied the invitation in his hand. He was stunned. "I've never dreamed of this! But there is no question of whether or not we should go."

A few weeks later, Dick was teaching the book of 1 Thessalonians to an audience of pastors in Tourane. "Paul the apostle speaks of his methodology of being that of a 'father and a mother,'" he said. "As spiritual parents, you teach your church by your own example. It is a method of visual aid. You are the visual aid. You teach your church to teach others. You make men and women into fishers of men."

Soon after the conference the mission was asked to send a missionary to assist the Vietnamese in the task of teaching men and women to evangelize and disciple. Again, the mission responded with a yes.

During the early years of the new mission, Dick recalled more about his Chinese work than just the evangelistic strategy. He remembered well the years of loneliness he had experienced in China while in the remote region of Honan province. He knew many missionaries faced the same sense of isolation and despair he had known, often going months or years at a time without the refreshment of spiritual teaching from other believers. They needed encouragement, a chance to see a face from home, an opportunity to rest from the rigors of preaching, teaching, and ministering. As a result, Orient Crusades took the uncommon step of designing activities to encourage and refresh missionaries.

"We are a service mission, and a nondenominational one at that. I believe the missionaries will trust us and allow us to minister to them," Dick challenged the Orient Crusades team. "We will arrange the speakers and hold the conferences. It must be a time of spiritual feeding for the missionaries. They need an opportunity to be convicted, encouraged, and stimulated. Our mission can do it!"

And so the first missionary conference was scheduled. Norman and Muriel Cook, a couple from Taylor University who had joined Orient Crusades staff, were the first hosts. Forty missionaries attended.

It was as Dick had predicted. The missionaries responded to the loving ministry of the Orient Crusades. Little gripes were aired and hurts mended. Time was spent in private confession of sin. The much-needed encouragement was served up in large portions, and the missionaries left feeling fed and refreshed, ready to return to their places of ministry. In time, the conferences drew hundreds.

As Orient Crusades developed, it encountered growing pains. Finances were often a struggle, and after many months only 10 percent of their budget was received. "But as long as there is flour for pancakes, none of us will starve to death," they assured each other, referring to the one dish almost anyone involved with Orient Crusades would have tasted.

Orient Crusades pancakes were famous. The young basketball players grew accustomed to sitting down to a stack after a big game in one of Taiwan's cities. If that was all there was, the athletes were glad to have it. It was a learning experience for those who sat to eat as well as those women at Taiwan's headquarters who, by faith, scraped together the ingredients and made them stretch to feed the big, hungry men. Dick often reminded himself, and the others, that, though they were working on a shoestring, "It is God's shoestring."

In spite of the financial difficulties, there were evidences of prosperity. The tiny staff grew to include college graduates with fresh enthusiasm for service and seasoned veterans of the missionary effort who were rich with experience and wisdom.

Young people joined to serve in the offices both in Los Angeles and in Taiwan. It was an eclectic group of personalities, backgrounds, church affiliations, ages, and races, all joined to serve Jesus Christ and His church.

The Orient Crusades moved into Hong Kong at the request of the church there, to train the people for the task of evangelizing and discipling their own countrymen. Stretching the dollars, energies, and too-short hours of each day, the team of missionaries continued their quest into the Orient.

In 1956, Orient Crusades was asked to consider participating in the missionary effort on the South American continent. Dick had never anticipated the ministry's setting foot beyond the beaches of Taiwan. He had never imagined stretching the sphere of ministry into the Western Hemisphere. The mission's name indicated that fact.

The challenge came from a young missionary from Argentina named Keith Bentson. He was impressed with the philosophy of ministry for which the mission was becoming widely known. He wanted to take to Argentina Orient Crusades' method of lay evangelism.

Dick considered himself an Oriental, from the "top of my head to the bottom of my feet!" He had lived more than a quarter of a century in the Oriental culture. Though he understood the truth that "God so loved the world," his own world had seldom extended beyond the Asian lands to which he had ministered so long.

Now he faced the opportunity to broaden the outreach and influence of this biblical principle he had proved with success in the Orient: train by example; teach national believers to witness and become disciplers; follow Christ's example of turning men into fishers of men.

Oswald Chambers, the great Bible scholar of the early 1900s, wrote, "There is no choice of service, only absolute obedience."

"There is no choice," Dick told the mission. "We must obey the call of God to go to Argentina."

As they prayed together about the venture into Argentina, they grew excited. Changes would have to be made. The name of the mission would have to go, if the mission were to continue to go "into the uttermost parts of the earth." And so Overseas Crusades was born.

Dick looked for someone to act as foreign director for the South American territory. His twin brother, Don, had just returned from missionary service in India. He stepped into the position, bringing all the years of experience accumulated since he had joined the missionary endeavor of TEAM [The Evangelical Alliance Mission] in 1936.

Prayers began to batter heaven for more workers to join the effort beginning in South America. Ed Murphy was one answer to those prayers. Dick heard him preach a sermon one Sunday in Pasadena, California. In his direct, forthright manner, Dick approached Ed and said, "That was a great message, but it should have been preached in South America, instead of California."

Ed was stunned. He knew it was providence—not coincidence—that put Dick in the congregation that day. "I must come see you," Ed responded, the excitement evident in his voice. "My wife and I have been burdened for South America. Maybe this is what God wants us to do."

At that time Ed was the pastor of a church in the San Fernando Valley. After many hours of prayer he was certain that he should leave the pastorate and join the growing family of missionaries now a part of Overseas Crusades. He took his wife and family and went to live and minister in Argentina. Later, he became field director for Argentina, and for Colombia when that country joined the others of the world that invited Overseas Crusades in to work with the national believers of the already existing churches.

With the mission's expansion into the South American countries, Dick knew he needed to become familiar and comfortable with their different cultures and peoples. He made his first trip to South America with Ray Stedman, a pastor and author from California who had taken a seat on the board of directors for the mission.

While in Argentina, Dick and Ray met a young national named Luis Palau. Luis was working and helping in the offices of Overseas Crusades. Dick and Ray were captivated by the vibrant young Argentine. His enthusiasm for the Scripture and his desire to know God and serve Him seemed boundless. He had a special spark of zeal for learning and sharing his faith with others.

Ray couldn't forget him. Even after he returned home to California he thought about Luis and began writing to him. He shared with his church the interest he had in this dynamic Argentine Christian and was encouraged by his congregation to offer help. He wrote and urged Luis, "Come to the States and attend Bible school. My church is willing to help you with tuition and registration costs. We'll do all we can to help you get here."

With the help of Ray Stedman's church, Luis came to the United States and enrolled in Multnomah School of the Bible. When he finished his courses he applied to Overseas Crusades. He and his wife, Pat, were accepted and assigned to Colombia, where Luis began his ministry of evangelism.

Dick and other leaders of the mission watched Luis's particular gifts grow—evangelism and Bible teaching. Under Ed Murphy's direction he led campaigns throughout Colombia. Luis's vision of ministry included the whole of the Spanish-speaking world, and in time the rest of the world as well.

Seeing the people of South America respond to the gospel of Jesus Christ was an experience that enlarged Dick's view of ministry. As he watched the message of salvation enter country after country and change lives, he grew more and more excited about the possibility of moving into other parts of the world. He began to see the need to be a "world Christian," and to challenge other believers to be "world Christians" too.

"This is like putting a wide-angle lens on and seeing the rest of the world," he said wherever he traveled. "It is because I have seen the people of South America respond that I recognize the whole world as a mission field. Now it doesn't matter where the door opens, I just want to be there and have workers there."

But behind every worker there must be a batallion of prayer supporters and financial contributors. There must be those who will attend to the details of the workers' lives while they attend to the work of preaching and teaching. So, while the work abroad grew, the responsibilities of the home office increased. The expansion from that sector was led by Norman Cummings. The home office provided the important services that made it possible for the missionaries to go and to stay on the fields that needed them.

Brazil was one of those needy fields. Dick received an invitation from the department of evangelism of the Presbyterian Church of Brazil to come and speak with the leaders of the church in that country. They had severed all relations with the Presbyterian Church of the U.S., but seven of the Brazilian church leaders gathered and wrote to Dick asking him to come and tell them about the work of the mission.

Dick knew it was to be a jury trial. The nationalistic spirit of Brazil was strong. The leaders of the Brazilian churches had no desire to come under the dictatorial rule of a foreign mission organization, yet they felt the need for help in their ministry to their people. They had heard of the philosophy of Overseas Crusades, and its methodology intrigued them. They assembled and asked Dick question after question about the mission, probing for every detail of its methods and goals.

Dick listened to each question and answered carefully, spelling out the motto of the mission. "We preach not ourselves, not our mission organization. Our desire is to help you, the church leaders of your own nation, to equip your laity to help in the work of evangelizing Brazil. As a mission, we are your servants, here to work with you, equipping the saints for the work of evangelists."

At the end of the grueling session of questions and answers, the mission was invited to come to Brazil.

With excitement, the mission prepared for its ministry in this new territory. As he considered different men for the position of field director, one young man's name kept coming to Dick's mind: Hans Wilhelm.

Hans was a teenager when Dick met him in 1947. He was living in Shanghai with missionary parents who were serving under a German arm of China Inland Mission. He attended a German high school and considered himself a loyal German. At one time he had been a member of the Hitler Youth Corps.

Germany's defeat in World War II had been a blow to young Hans. His personal turmoil was evident to Dick, who had begun to take special notice of the teenager. When the CIM families in Shanghai gathered together to study the Bible and pray on Sunday afternoons, Dick took time to talk with Hans. He challenged him to begin memorizing passages of the Bible. He encouraged him to memorize the entire book of Philippians. Hans accepted the challenge and memorized the four chapters of the New Testament epistle. He soon began studying and memorizing other parts of the Bible. As his knowledge increased his faith grew. The Savior of whom his parents preached became real to him.

Hans began to sense within himself a growing love for Jesus. His desire to obey Him began to cast shadows on the philosophy of the Hitler Youth Movement that had at one time been so important to him. The godless values of the Nazi system could not be reconciled with the relationship he now enjoyed with Jesus. He soon released all lingering interest in the Nazi philosophy and aligned himself completely with the Christ of the Bible.

In 1950, when communist guns forced them out of China, the two missionary families found themselves together on the refugee ship, the *General Gordon*, for the nightmare voyage to America. The Wilhelms settled in Nebraska after a short visit to their homeland, and Dick's ministry to Chiang kai-Shek's defeated troops soon took him to Taiwan.

But Dick never lost interest in the young German he had been so drawn to in Shanghai. While in California on mission business he stopped to see the young man, who was then a student at UCLA.

Dick told him of the work going on in Taiwan and the way God had brought a new mission organization into existence.

"When are you going to come and help us, Hans?" he asked him.

Dick had seen in Hans a quick responsiveness to the work of personal evangelism and discipleship. He could visualize that spark growing into a strong flame and burning brightly on Taiwan. But the time wasn't right. After graduation from UCLA, Hans joined the staff of Navigators, and under their tutelage his gifts of evangelism and discipling flourished. Soon he was again confronted with a request from Dick Hillis.

Dick contacted the Navigators organization and asked, "Could you send some young men from your staff to work with us in the discipleship program here on Taiwan?"

And he asked specifically for Hans Wilhelm.

Soon after the request was made Hans arrived in Taiwan. He was anxious to see his friend again and become involved in the work on the island country. The conversations the two had enjoyed in earlier years resumed: Dick often counseling, Hans listening and learning, both encouraging each other. When Hans's interest in Alice, Dick's secretary, became evident, the conversations took a different turn.

"Hans, be sure of the mate you choose. God will direct you, but be patient. Your wife can make a difference in your ministry. Be sure she is the woman God has for you."

Hans listened and agreed to be prayerful and patient. The story of Dick's own patient, prayerful wait for Margaret was well-known to him. Three years later he married Alice and left Navigators to become an official member of the staff of Oriental Crusades.

Dick once wrote to Hans, "You've influenced every life you've touched: either toward Christ, or away from Him." Hans could not escape the impact of that statement. He carried it with him as a continual challenge.

Though his heart was in foreign mission work, Hans returned to the States with his family and began studying at Fuller Seminary. It was while he was in California that Dick again confronted him with another request.

"I'd like to spend some time with you, Hans," Dick spoke into the phone. "Could we meet and talk awhile?"

"I've got something to talk over with you too, Dick," Hans answered his friend. "Where and when?"

The men agreed to meet in Hisperia and talk over what seemed to each of them the unlikely direction in which God appeared to be leading.

"What I've got to say is pretty 'way out,'" Dick began, yet before he could say more, Hans laughed.

"Wait until you hear what I've got to say!"

"Well, then," answered a curious Dick, "you go first."

Hans began, "Dick, I know this is going to sound crazy, but I think God may be calling me to minister in Brazil."

Dick could hardly believe his ears.

"I know I speak Mandarin, and I grew up in the Oriental culture and have ministered there for years, but I think God is asking me to take up a new challenge in South America. What do you think?"

"That's exactly why I've come to see you, Hans. We've been asked to send a team to Brazil to work with the national church. As I've prayed about who to send as field director, yours is the only name that has come to my mind. I came to see you today to ask you if you would consider going to Brazil!"

As the two men looked at each other, awe and amazement brought grins to their faces. Chuckling, they agreed it didn't make sense, but then, since when have finite minds fully understood the infinite thoughts and plans of God?

Hans and his family left for Brazil to take up the position of leadership needed there. When the work was well established, Hans answered another challenge for the Overseas Crusades and went to Germany to lead a team in the work of the church of his homeland.

For most of the years since they met, continents and oceans separated Hans and Dick. Yet friendship thrived. Letters traveled the circumference of the globe, carrying encouragement and the news of God's work in whatever country they happened to be. Time and travel have caused the welcomed letters to become lost or discarded. But one remains, a reminder of the value of time invested in a young life:

> Dear Dick,
>   I just want to thank you for the times of laughter and tears. Your impact on my life cannot be measured this side of heaven.
>   Hans

22

Passages

"God is looking for men on whom He can put the weight of all His love and power and faithfulness," A. B. Simpson wrote. Dick Hillis seemed to be such a man. The weight of God's love and power and faithfulness drove him on, causing him to seek men and women who would carry that weight with him. He sought recruits, raised support for the work and the workers, traveled to encourage the missionaries in the God-appointed task of making disciples of all the nations.

His passion for the health of the local churches increased. Since the days of his youthful ambitions in China, experience and wisdom had accumulated. His understanding of the needs of the local churches grew. He now thought of himself as one concerned for the whole world.

With the addition of the South American countries, not only had the focus of the mission broadened, but so had Dick's. And following close on the heels of growth came change. From a more central location Dick could better administrate the now widespread and rapidly growing ministries of the once tiny organization that had called itself the Formosa Gospel Crusades. The time had come to move the headquarters of the mission from Taiwan to California.

The move from Taiwan to the States was, in some ways, a painful one for the Hillis family. During the ten years they had lived in Taiwan the children had come to love it as their home. On the tiny mission compound the Overseas Crusades staff families lived near each other, and close relationships evolved. Though Dick's work required much traveling, Margaret and the children were surrounded continually by the other missionary families.

There was a sense of continuity to the family life, due in large part to Margaret's steady presence, even though Dick was often away for weeks at a time. Living among other members of the Overseas Crusades families helped to give the six Hillis children a sharp sense of belonging to the total work of the mission their father had founded. Each child was helped to feel a part of Dick's ministry, whether he was at home or in a country many miles from Taiwan.

Leaving the island country meant leaving that intimate environment of loving friends, but in 1962 the move was accomplished. Dick, as general director, would be better able to ensure that the entire mission functioned with the vision and mandate with which it had been established. His main task became conducting conferences and seminars for his own missionaries, and pastor's conferences for national pastors and lay leaders.

"The health of a church in large measure depends upon the health of the pastor," he stated again and again as he spoke to pastors, regardless of their denomination. He urged them to be revived, to be "visual aids" and models of the life and ministry of Christ, to lead their churches by their own example.

"The national church is the answer to evangelism," he reiterated. "On your face and mine will always be the 'Made in U.S.A.' stamp. The number of vital *Christians* in a country is the key, *not* the number of missionaries!"

With each mile of territory he traveled, Dick's intensity for the message increased. But in 1963 all was suddenly interrupted by a doctor's command: "You must have eye surgery."

It was delicate surgery. The man of seemingly inexhaustible energy had to lie still under a surgeon's knife. The first operation was successful: the removal of one lens. The second, some months later, was disastrous. A slip of the doctor's knife cut the iris and scarred the retina. For weeks Dick feared he would be blind in that eye, that he might even have to give up the work that was his life. Once before he had been forced out of the ministry he loved by the point of a communist rifle. Now it was the point of a surgeon's scalpel that threatened to force him out.

Eventually, Dick's prayers for his sight were answered. He was fitted with glasses, and with the use of a contact lens the vision in one eye was corrected to 20/20. The injured eye was left with peripheral vision.

As soon as the doctor pronounced him well enough, he returned to his work. The fact that his eyesight was impaired did not diminish his vision for world evangelism.

The mission's influence continued to expand. The mission that had suddenly found itself on the South American continent found itself just as suddenly in the European country of Greece.

Paul the apostle once wrote to a church in Greece, in the city of Thessalonica. Twenty centuries later Christians in that same city wrote to Overseas Crusades asking for someone to come and train their people to witness and disciple others. They asked specifically for a man of Greek background who knew the language and the culture.

In response, the mission family prayed for God's choice for the church in Thessalonica. Later, while Dick was at a missions conference in Boston, he met a young Greek named Michael Kantartjis.

"I'm pastoring a large Greek assembly here in Boston," Michael told Dick as they visited together one afternoon. "But my deep desire is to go to Greece and minister to my own people in the country of my heritage."

Dick's interest was piqued. He listened with excitement as Michael went on. "I'm especially interested in serving in the area of Berea and Thessalonica," the young pastor said.

He was interviewed and accepted by the mission. In 1966 Greece was added to the number of countries that had enlisted the aid of the growing service organization established for ten dollars in Washington, D.C., just fifteen years earlier.

The sixties also saw the Overseas Crusades missionaries invited into Mexico and Indonesia. Luis Palau, the young Argentine, began to travel extensively throughout the Spanish-speaking countries. A trained group of counselors joined him, and the Luis Palau Evangelistic Team evolved. The vast magnitude of that new ministry thrilled the mission. Luis emerged as a dominant personality in the world of evangelism. Thousands of Spanish-speaking people responded to the fiery young man. Many compared him to the now world-famous evangelist, Billy Graham. The power of the Holy Spirit generated intensity and enthusiasm that drew crowds of thousands wherever he spoke.

Growth was present wherever Overseas Crusades went. Churches in the islands of Indonesia swelled with new believers. And because of the discipleship emphasis of the work, maturity characterized the lives of those under the OC ministry.

Every gift available was used in the work of discipling and evangelism. The Singing Ambassador, Norman Nelson, ministered through music. Overseas Ambassadors, a layman's division of the mission, carried out its objective of engaging laymen in witnessing.

Although the mission moved forward, active forces attempted to hinder and destroy. The decade of the sixties, which saw such great success, was also witness to struggle and destruction. Loud anti-American voices shouted in many of the countries where Overseas Crusades ministered.

In Ecuador, anti-American feelings were at a feverish peak. Such were the conditions when the Sports Ambassadors basketball team arrived. Only weeks earlier the visit of an American official had sparked riots in which five people were killed. On the eve of the scheduled game the American embassy warned them, "You play this game at your own risk. We cannot protect or defend you should a riot occur."

The game was played to a packed stadium despite signs reading "Yankee go home!" The game started well, although every six minutes officials had to stop the game to give the U.S. players oxygen because of the high altitude. They were behind by eight points at the half, but the spectators sat silent during the halftime program and listened to the message of faith in Jesus Christ.

During the last twenty minutes of the game the audience cheered for the American team. Such a thing had never happened before in Ecuador's athletic history. Though the Sports Ambassadors lost the game by one point, they described it as a victory. Eight hundred fifty people responded to the offer of a free Bible correspondence course. Three hours after the game was over, people were still standing and listening, wanting to know more about the Christ the players had spoken of.

Other contests elsewhere in the world were not so easily won, the rules not so clearly defined. Such was true of the gory, bitter struggle raging in another of Overseas Crusades fields. The country of Vietnam lay bleeding and dying under the continual assault of the communist Viet Cong.

"Terrorism here in Tuyen Duc province has greatly increased since the bombing halt and expanded peace talks," the missionaries wrote home.

Glenn Johnson's letter described the premeditated murders that took place in one seven-day period, just footsteps from his home. The year 1969 found Vietnam's Overseas Crusades missionaries and national believers holding out little hope for peace.

Glenn's report read: "Sunday—V.C. squad detonated huge satchel of plastic explosives in the basement of a retired colonel's home. A member of the Dalat House of Representatives, the colonel and his wife and eleven children were asleep in the house. Three of them will never awaken. In the night we could hear the screams of those who survived but could do nothing to help them.

"This is communist strategy—maneuvering in Paris, murdering in South Vietnam. Their goal? To deprive South Vietnam of its government leadership. That totally innocent men, women and children are killed to gain this goal is immaterial. Such is godless atheism."

Yet the work continued. John Newman and his wife, Jo, and the Johnsons and the believers there saw victories in the lives of individuals, though they observed defeat in the war effort.

Glenn ended his letter from Vietnam with the words, "Hard-pressed on every side, we are never hemmed in; bewildered, we are never at our wits' end; hunted, we are never abandoned to our fate; struck down, we are not left to die" (2 Corinthians 4:8-9, NEB*).

They carried on the ministry in the military hospitals, in small village gatherings, wherever there were people. During one seven-day period services were held for over a thousand Vietnamese soldiers. Their message: peace and hope through Jesus, the Man of Sorrows.

Many thousands of miles from the war zone, Dick and Margaret fought their own personal battle concerning Vietnam. Brian, their youngest son, was determined to join the Marines and fight in that bloody war. While his parents prayed he would change his mind, Brian asked God to allow him to enlist and be sent to Vietnam.

Releasing their son to God's will was far from easy for Dick and Margaret, but they knew faith required it. After weeks of anxious prayers and frustration, they finally acknowledged to each other, "We've got to allow Brian to seek the guidance of the Lord himself. We can't tell him what God wants him to do."

Brian entered the Marines and completed boot camp. The day before he was to be shipped to Vietnam his papers were lost. He was sent to North Carolina to await assignment in the Carribean although his company was sent to the war zone, where many of them died.

In the years after his discharge from the Marine Corps, Brian studied in North Carolina and helped to start a Bible study at the university. The study grew and later became part of the foundation of a church numbering a thousand people. Brian's penchant for challenge did not subside. With his university degree in special education, he joined the ranks of world missions and headed toward Colombia to work with handicapped children.

While Brian was contemplating his place in the world, the older daughters of the Hillis family, Margaret Anne and Nancy, married. The Hillis home gradually emptied of children. Marriage as well as missionary interests drew the children into lives of their own.

As Dick watched the changes taking place around him, he began to consider the possibility of making some changes himself. It had been twenty

New English Bible.

years since Overseas Crusades had come into life. It was time to stand back and assess its strength and its needs. It was time for evaluating. Just as his position as father to his children had changed through twenty years of parenting, so his role as founder of the mission had changed. He wondered if it was time for letting go, releasing, as he had had to do with his children.

23

A Time to Weep

It was the beginning of a new decade. And with it came new beginnings for Dick. For months he had felt growing frustration. There wasn't enough time for all that he wanted to do. He felt a compulsion to spend more time with his missionaries, with native pastors, to encourage those who were laboring in the fields for the cause of the gospel. Though he scheduled pastors' conferences and seminars for missionaries, the duties required of him as general director limited the time he could spend in those areas. It was time to be freed from papers and mission politics to give more time to the needs of people. In 1971 he asked to be released from the administrative responsibilities of his position as general director.

That meant someone must be appointed to take responsibility for the overall administration of the mission's operations from the headquarters, which were now located in Palo Alto, California. There was no debate over Dick's successor. There could be only one choice: Norman Cummings.

Norm and his wife, Amy, had been with Overseas Crusades for twenty years. In 1954 they had moved into "the Mansion"—a huge, old house that served as both office and mission home. When OC missionaries returned to the states, Amy welcomed them into the Mansion and was hostess, cook, and friend during their stay. Norm spent years filling every vacancy that occurred within the mission staff. His energies were poured into every area of the mission's functions. He was printer, carpenter, personnel director, and often packer for the travel-weary missionary who came through the Mansion.

No one was more qualified for the position as executive director than Norman Cummings. No one was more familiar with the running of the mission—from the most basic functions of the plumbing in the Mansion to the most intricate complications of foreign visa requirements.

With the administrative reins in Norm's hands, Dick began to travel more extensively and do the things he loved most: preach, encourage the missionaries, and observe the workings of the mission in order to report to the board of directors and to the many churches and individuals who supported its work.

With great excitement he reported the mission's continuing advances into the uttermost parts of the earth. An invitation came from the church in the city-nation of Singapore. Overseas Crusades missionaries went to teach the believers there to disciple and evangelize their own people, and a spirit of celebration surged within the organization as another field joined the swelling ranks of the Overseas Crusades family. But the taste of celebration quickly turned bittersweet as reports poured in from Vietnam, telling of the war's escalation and the killing of more thousands.

Dick scheduled a trip to minister to the pastors in that troubled field. He traveled as far as Bangkok, then attempted to book passage to Saigon. Through ham radio contact with the American Embassy in that city he learned that getting into the country could be easily accomplished, but flights out of Saigon were booked up for three months. The city was packed with refugees trying to escape. If he went in, it would be impossible to get back out again.

"For goodness sake, don't come in!" the ham radio operator shouted. The concern and urgency in his voice traveled through the static of the radio. "We are going to have to evacuate all the missionaries. We will be lucky to get them all out safely. Don't come in!"

Dick was stunned. Though he knew the conditions in that small, war-ravaged country were desperate, he had not expected this. He remembered his own flight from a war-torn country years earlier, and he knew his missionaries would be reluctant to leave the land they had come to love as home and the people they had learned to love as brothers and sisters. He knew the message he had to send to his missionaries: Get out.

He knew the words would cut their souls. He recalled the rebellion he had felt many years earlier when mission administrators had told him he must leave China's inland province of Honan. He remembered in minute detail the sensations of fear and horror he had experienced when communist soldiers shouted, "Get out!" Now he had no choice, however, but to say the same words. Tears choked him as he gripped the radio microphone tightly. He drew a deep breath and spoke the order that he knew would carry crushing grief to his friends.

"Tell them to get out of the country. I will meet them in Hong Kong."

One by one, family by family, the missionaries were evacuated to Hong Kong. They stepped from the planes, dazed and exhausted from the trauma of their escape. Dick greeted each one with hugs and tears and said gently, "I'm proud of you. You've done well."

For the next few days the missionaries stayed in Hong Kong, waiting for energy and strength to return and awaiting flights for home. During those days the stories of their escape and their efforts to help their Christian friends escape unfolded.

As Dick listened he felt his pride in them swell—pride for their courage, their stamina, and their devotion to their Savior and His people in that sad country. Because of their valor several of the Koho tribespeople, the Children of the Mountains, had been helped out of the country to safety. Many Christian Chinese had been aided in their flight by the missionaries whose own safety was jeopardized every moment they delayed their own flight.

Dick shared with them the story of his own flight from China when the Communists had forced him out of the country at gunpoint. When anger surged through his friends, he understood and soothed them. He added his tears to their tears of disappointment. Together they mourned for the country that had had so little time to learn of the Prince of Peace, for the people who had died at the hands of godless aggressors and for the work that was so suddenly ended.

Years later Dick would say that the fall of Vietnam and the closing of that field was the most shattering event in the history of the mission. Yet years later he would still be marveling at the providence of God that had placed him there in the Orient at the time when the missionaries were forced out. When they needed the comfort and assurance that their ministry was not all in vain, God placed Dick among them as the living example of what can be built out of seemingly broken pieces.

"I know what you are suffering," he told the missionaries. "I am feeling it all over again with you—all the same pain and grief I felt when China was lost to me. I was numb, as though there was no reality except the reality of God's sovereignty. Only the remembrance of that helped to assuage the pain. Listen to these words." And he opened his Bible and read to them from the prophet Habakkuk.

Though the fig tree should not blossom, and there be no fruit on the vines,
Though the yield of the olive should fail, and the fields produce no food,

Though the flock should be cut off from the fold, and there be no cattle in the
   stalls,
Yet will I exult in the Lord, I will rejoice in the God of my salvation.
                                                          (Habakkuk 3:17-18, NASB*)

And he read them David's words, "He is the Lord our God; His judgments
are in all the earth" (Psalm 105:7, NASB).

Together they prayed for the believers left behind in the villages and cities
and farming areas of Vietnam. Their lives would be in great danger once the
communist regime firmly established itself.

Glenn Johnson was especially concerned for two national believers who
had worked closely with him in his ministry to the military personnel.
Daniel and Diane Tran had not been evacuated with the others. They were
somewhere in that war-torn country. The relief the missionaries felt at their
own safety was marred by their concern for those left behind. Not until word
came through that the Trans had escaped did the missionaries allow
themselves to relax in their own safety.

Once safely out of the country, the Trans made their way to America.
There they contacted the Overseas Crusades office. Within a short time they
were welcomed to the mission staff and resumed their ministry with their
own people, sharing the message of the Prince of Peace with the 130,000
dispersed Vietnamese then in the United States.

Dick met still another sorrow in the aftermath of the fall of Vietnam.
Before he could return home from his aborted trip to Vietnam, he received
word that his friend General Chiang kai-Shek had died. Immediately, he flew
to Taipei, Taiwan.

In the early days of his ministry in Taiwan Dick had said, "One of the
greatest joys I have experienced is the growing friendship with President and
Madame Chiang. I am convinced that they are truly believers in Jesus Christ.

"It is a great joy to have the freedom to discuss spiritual things, to
correspond with them, to have dinner in their home. These have been vital
experiences," he wrote twenty years earlier.

Words written twenty centuries earlier spoke comfort to the deceased
president's family, friends, and the island nation he led: "For I am
persuaded, that neither death, nor life, nor angels, nor principalities, nor
powers, nor things present, nor things to come, nor height, nor depth, nor
any other creature, shall be able to separate us from the love of God, which is
in Christ Jesus our Lord" (Romans 8:38-39).

*New American Standard Bible.

24

Decade of Determination

The years of the 1970s could well be described as the decade of determination, for during that time the work of Overseas Crusades escalated with almost fierce determination. No country was too small or insignificant to be overlooked; no land too remote to be denied aid to its churches. And there was no limit to the number of people hungry for the Bread of Life.

This was seen in the continually growing masses that thronged to stadiums, sports arenas, and civic centers to hear the now world-recognized evangelist, Luis Palau. Backed by his team of counselors and the follow-up workers, Luis's ministry spanned the South American and Central American countries and began to launch out into the rest of the world.

The first European Youth Conference was held in Brussels, Belgium, the city recognized by the Common Market countries as the capital of Europe. Luis joined hands with Billy Graham to preach to eight thousand young people from thirty countries. Christians around the world viewed "Eurofest '75" as the beginning of a spiritual awakening in Europe.

Meanwhile, on the South American continent, the Vencadores por Cristo (Victors for Christ) shared the beauty of the Christian life through the medium of music. Nationals, selected from universities and churches on the basis of their musical ability and spiritual commitment, spent several weeks in intensive Bible study. They trained for public sharing, small group counseling, and practiced their music hundreds of hours. Their finely tuned presentations of blended voices and instruments spread the "happy news."

Their records sold throughout the countries, and local radios played their albums over the air waves. Broadcasting stations played video tapes of their musical performances to the masses of television viewers.

The mission's twenty-fifth birthday came in 1976 and was a year of celebration. It was a time for retrospect too, but a short time only. The founder was too busy looking ahead to the next twenty-five years to spare more than a thankful, cursory look backward. The *Cable,* Overseas Crusades' "house organ," reviewed the founder's early "China Years" and told of the way Dick had come upon the philosophy for ministry among his Chinese friends in the distant Honan province—the philosophy that later became the mandate for the mission he founded.

The final pages of the *Cable* stated, "We ask God if it please Him, to place OC missionaries in every free nation in the world 'in the next 25. . . .'

"While it took centuries for the world population to reach the first billion people, it took only fifteen years to add the next billion . . . And in another short fifteen years the world population will increase another billion people . . . So it is necessary that the growth of the mission be accelerated."

It was an ambitious goal. Changes would have to be made if it was to be realized. One such change was the decision to establish the office of a president of the mission. Prayerfully the board of directors considered who might be God's choice for the position. Always in prayer and discussion the young Argentine, Luis Palau, was prominent. When offered the position of president of Overseas Crusades, Luis accepted.

His leadership abilities would be placed out in front of the mission; his energy and enthusiasm would set a new pace for them all. His acceptance as a world figure would also be a valuable asset to the work of the mission.

At his inauguration in January 1977, Luis said, "We want to preach Christ Jesus fully to every person in the nations the Father opens to us by stimulating and mobilizing the Body of Christ to continuous, effective evangelism, and church multiplication on a nation-wide basis, so millions will be transformed into victorious Christians."

It was a huge undertaking, the task of evangelizing the world, but Dick was convinced that with the proper use of all forms of mass media, OC could play a significant part in helping believers reach the whole world in the present generation.

Reach the whole world! Dick felt a sense of awe grow inside him as he considered such a vision. Who could have known that the glimpse of 1.5 million Chinese in a small county in the heart of mainland China would grow to such proportions? It was a staggering goal to the mind that did not take into account the power of God, the "Nothing-He-Cannot-Do-One."

Dick's own personal goals remained much the same. With Luis in the leadership role as president, he continued to focus his attention on Bible conferences, missionary refreshment seminars, and, when time permitted, pursued a growing interest in writing and radio work for the mission.

"I am rejoicing that God has raised up Luis and a strong supportive leadership team for the mission," he wrote to the family of missionaries and supporters throughout the world. "I will continue to work closely with them in developing the forward growth of the mission."

The support team Dick referred to consisted of Hans Wilhelm, who accepted the position of executive vice-president; Norman Cummings, executive director; Norman Cook, divisional director of Asia; Chuck Holsinger, divisional director of U.S. Ministries; Paul Landrey, divisional director of Colombia; and Bill Keyes, divisional director of Brazil.

In all, the team provided a sum of over one hundred years' experience in the world of missions. They were anxious to move out further in worldwide mission. The ministry that began in China now circled the globe. Like the British Empire of the nineteenth century, it could be said, the sun never set on Overseas Crusades.

The first winter after his inauguration, Luis teamed with Billy Graham for a five-day crusade in Manila, Philippines. Over half a million Filipinos attended, and of that number 20,000 responded to the invitation to receive the salvation provided in Jesus Christ. Millions more listened to the message of God's gift on nationwide radio and television. Comprehensive reports on the crusades filled the newspapers. Pastors, 5,100 strong, participated in a school for evangelism. It was a great harvest, but only the beginning, the first step toward the fulfillment of the dream to see the whole world evangelized.

The determination to reach the ends of the earth with the message of the Good News surged after the tremendous response the mission saw in the Philippines. With vigor and enthusiasm the mission inaugurated the Overseas Crusades of Canada, Inc., that same winter of 1977. It was launched through missions conferences and other ministries in churches, colleges, and seminaries. Canadian young people were challenged to become the vanguard of a host of missionaries to the yet unevangelized world.

The winter of 1977 also saw a very personal battle in the Hillis home in Santa Clara, California. Dick and Margaret began a determined fight against physical illness. Margaret was diagnosed as having breast cancer.

Years earlier, while Margaret was in her thirties, a tumor was removed from her breast. Later, in 1975, a problem had reappeared but was diagnosed as scar tissue. A year later, the same problem still troubled her, and Margaret made a more determined effort to satisfy her concern. A thorough examination was made and a biopsy of the tissue conducted.

In December, Dick phoned the children with the results: Mom had cancer. What was reckoned as scar tissue had all along been a malignancy. Immediate radical surgery was required. But the cancer was already in an advanced stage, and the doctors could make no sure prognosis. Treatment and chemotherapy began at once. The battle against the disease waged with full force.

While Dick and Margaret engaged in the war against cancer, new combat ideas were being developed for fighting Satan's forces elsewhere in the world. New methods of dispelling spiritual darkness were being tried in Africa.

It was well known that the Sports Ambassadors had made a name for themselves in the world of basketball, but that held little interest for the citizens of Lesotho, a recently formed nation of Africa. Their national sport was soccer.

"So let's form a soccer team!" was the battle cry from Bud Schaeffer, Overseas Crusades sports director. So in 1978, a Christian soccer team went to Africa—the first time in the history of sports that a soccer team officially represented the United States in Africa.

The new soccer team won enough games to receive high praise from government and sports officials. A national pastor reported that "soccer in Christian shoes is a 'more excellent way' to reach some of the semi-closed Muslim nations of Africa for Christ."

The president of Swaziland Sports Federation, a Christian, said, "Your coming is a gift from heaven."

The praise for the soccer team was accompanied by an invitation to return.

Not all the reports from the battle zones around the world were as exciting and pleasing as this, however. David Liao, Overseas Crusades missionary to Thailand, wrote of the murder and devastation crushing the country of Cambodia. His years with OC had well qualified him as a mission leader, but nothing had prepared him for the slaughter he observed in Cambodia. "The Communists are exterminating their own race," he wrote. "Half the population has been murdered or has fled to other countries. It is believed that over six thousand believers have been murdered. But in such great loss, many are turning to Christ."

Yet joy in the midst of sorrow was his message to his fellow missionaries. Success in the face of failure, victory in the place of defeat. The paradox of the Christian faith is nowhere better understood than in the mind of the believer who has witnessed the worst the enemy can do while experiencing the best that God can do.

In 1978 Norman Cummings retired after twenty-five years of service and leadership. He had successfully recovered from one heart attack a few years earlier, but the possibility of another loomed heavy above him, and so he retired from his post as executive director.

Another change followed quickly. Luis Palau's schedule and the demands of evangelism made it impossible for him to continue on in the position as president of the mission. He felt God was directing him to give his full time and energy to world evangelism.

After two years of service to the organization as the chief executive he wrote to the board, "We realize it will be impossible to continue to move into all the many avenues the Lord is opening to us around the world in mass evangelism while at the same time attending to the tremendous task of the ever-expanding missionary outreach of Overseas Crusades."

"I hated losing him," Dick said of Luis's resignation. "But you do not lose men to the will of God. You only lose men to sin."

Dick had struggled with "losing men" many times. During the beginning years of the mission's life Dick had had to let his own brother go. Though Don was an integral part of the mission's outreach, he left to rejoin TEAM as its associate general director.

Overseas Crusades did not just "let Luis go," they gave him several men from the OC staff and helped them give birth to the Luis Palau Evangelistic Team.

With Overseas Crusades' blessing, the new team took its first breaths of life. It was not long before the young organization was able to operate on its own. Another organ within the Body of Christ began exercising the power of God throughout the ends of the earth.

What appeared as loss emerged as gain. By launching Luis into a separate ministry, OC provided the platform by which world evangelism would increase in dimension and impact. Letting go meant going forward with the goal of the mission as stated at the 25th anniversary celebration: "help the whole body reach the whole world in our generation."

Though the leadership changed, the purpose of the mission never faltered or varied. Dick's own devotion to the Master's method remained strong. And though he had relinquished the administrative "paperwork," he remained a substantial force in the government of the organization he founded. Never relegated to the position of a figurehead, he modeled the servant attitude that had brought the mission into being.

"Don't tell your church to go [into all the world]—use Jesus' own example, 'come.' Lead the Body of Christ by your own example." He said it; he preached it; he insisted upon its being lived by the men who were considered for leadership roles within the structure of the organization.

In 1979 a new president stepped into the seat of the chief officer. Clyde Cook was a tall, gangly young man when he first met the Overseas Crusades group. He was a basketball player and fourth generation "missionary kid." His athletic accomplishments had been remarkable, yet he turned down thirteen scholarship offers in favor of attending Bible school. In 1963 he and his wife, Anna Belle, joined the Overseas Crusades staff and served in the Philippines until 1967. An alumnus of Biola, Talbot, and Fuller Theological Seminary, Dr. Cook brought to the mission not only mission knowledge and the credentials of education, but firsthand experience in field life.

Overseas Crusades' *World Spotlight,* a news magazine of the mission, wrote of him: "He is a man who sets goals, a man of prayer, strong in administration, a godly man with a warm presence about him, a man who deals honestly and forthrightly with issues and with others." The board of directors and staff welcomed him and his family to the fellowship of the mission.

There was a feeling of celebration that year of 1979. There was joy over the new president. And there was hope and anticipation for Dick and Margaret. The treatments and prayers had been effective, the doctors said. Margaret was free from cancer. She was well.

"I am glad to be off chemotherapy and am trusting Him daily," she wrote in a letter to the mission family. She was eager to report on the activities of her six children and to update her friends on her own progress. Her letter flowed like the lyrics of a song as she sang of her children's lives—all married and seeking God for themselves.

She closed with a quotation from Isaiah 12-2: "The Lord Jehovah is my strength and my song." It was evident she was enjoying a new awareness of life and its special pleasures.

Margaret's fight with cancer, the change in organizational leadership, and expansion into new countries were only some of the changes Overseas Crusades faced. Earlier in the decade the mission had moved its headquarters down the coast from Palo Alto to Santa Clara. They had seen the addition of Guatamala, France, India, Sri Lanka, and Australia to the ever-increasing number of lands where Overseas Crusades ministered.

25

God and a Girl

"It was a mistake."

The doctor's words were spoken carefully, but their impact was not quite clear for the first moments after they were uttered. Then, as the reality penetrated with a stinging point, the listeners understood.

"Margaret is not free from cancer."

She never was. During the nine months in which she received no treatment, the disease was steadily advancing, moving toward the ultimate destruction.

It was like the second devastating wave of a storm after a teasing calm has settled. Disbelief flooded and tore at the Hillises' senses. Hatred of the very word *cancer* welled up like a bitter gall. The war was not over as Dick and Margaret had believed. The weapons had to be picked up again, but this time the momentum was on the side of the enemy.

In October 1980, Dick wrote, "Margaret has just gone through a most difficult month but is now on the way up, and in answer to prayer is daily gaining strength. I feel that I am living with an answer to prayer. We are rejoicing together."

It was impossible for Dick and Margaret to conceive of God's taking her in death to leave Dick alone. Though he did not allow himself to get angry at God for Margaret's suffering, he also never allowed himself to believe that she would die from the disease. For Dick, life without Margaret was inconceivable. She was the magnetic pole around which the Hillis family rotated.

"If anything good has happened to the children it is primarily because of God and a girl," Dick said of the quiet, gentle woman he married.

Though Dick had set the pace for the spiritual walk in the family, it was Margaret who had maintained it. She had urged the children over the hurdles in the path, and made sure they understood the direction the family was headed. Her steady commitment to Dick and the ministry of the mission helped the children deal with the changes and challenges of being "MKs" (missionary kids).

Dick's position with the mission required weeks, months of travel each year. Yet his daughter, Nancy Lundsgaard, once said, "I don't remember being aware as a child that he was gone a lot." The patterns established while he was home were carried on in his absence by Margaret. There were no sudden stops or starts, no switch from a matriarchy to a patriarchy and back again. There was no detour from the road, no sense of being lost or abandoned. Margaret was the spiritual and physical center of the children's lives, always a stable force in the middle of a family who had at its head a world traveler. She maintained a continuity of family life that was essential to the children's security and stability. And she was the pivot point of Dick's life.

For forty-one years she had been his closest friend, his lover and companion. He was sure God would heal her. Margaret was sure. Together they prayed for it; they believed it; they expected a miracle of healing.

More than forty years earlier, in China, Dick had relinquished his bride to God, much as Abraham had surrendered to the same Lord the destiny of his precious son, Isaac. More than forty years earlier Dick had seen God restore his wife from a raging fever, much as Abraham had seen God restore Isaac to him by the provision of a ram in a nearby thicket. So now Dick waited for the "Nothing-He-Cannot-Do-One" to again restore the woman He had chosen for Dick. The aging Bible scholar kept one eye on his wife and one eye on the watch for the ram in the thicket, the way of escape God had so faithfully provided before.

But there was no ram.

Christmas 1980 was a special time for the Hillis family. For the first time in sixteen years the entire family was together for the holidays. From North Carolina, Illinois, Washington, and Southern California they gathered. The fourteen adults and thirteen grandchildren celebrated what was to be their last family gathering with Margaret.

Though others refused to accept the possibility of her death, Margaret, it seems, had begun to believe that her healing would come by way of her shedding the body that was so weak, for she understood that death is itself a healing.

"It was a never-to-be-forgotten time and we treasure every happy memory," she wrote of the reunion. "Our family is a great joy to us. We realize that with three families going overseas (to serve as missionaries and teachers) it is unlikely that we will ever meet together again down here. But it is wonderful to know we can spend eternity together with the Lord we love. As you pray for us, please remember the family."

In January 1981, Dick sent word to the mission family that "the last ninety days have been filled with triumphs and trials. Margaret went through four-and-a-half weeks of radiation in her battle against cancer. She took it well and the Lord has given her strength."

But that strength was ebbing, and in February Dick stopped his traveling altogether to be home with Margaret. He left her only during the daytime, and then always in the care of loving friends. He returned evenings to care for her himself and celebrate her companionship.

By March he wrote, "As I write this, Margaret is confined to bed and wheelchair, so I'm cook, cleaner, and chief bottle washer. After all her years of service to me, I count it a joy to serve her. It's also been a joy to have three of our children (John, Margaret Anne, and Nancy) take turns visiting to share not only the chores, but also their love for their mother."

Dick was no stranger to housework. He had never had a phobia of "women's work." His daughter, Nancy, told of their growing up years when he would stand at the foot of the stairs and call all the children down to "get organized" to get the housework done on Saturday mornings.

"When we were little he fed and bathed us," she reminisced. "He did dishes most of the time, housecleaning most of the time, but he never learned to cook at all."

Though pathetic in the kitchen, Dick did not give up. He continually coaxed Margaret to eat and tried to prepare whatever she wished. He handled the routine of her care with accustomed authority and ability, but it troubled Margaret to be waited on and cared for so totally. She tried to spare him as much as possible, smooth the way for the tasks.

Her one consuming concern was that he needed her. If she clung to any hope for healing it was for that reason only.

If Margaret's primary concern was for Dick's well-being, her secondary concern had always been for her children—and now for her grandchildren. During her last spring, she often spoke of her hope that she would be able to meet her 14th grandchild—due on April 21 to Jennifer, the youngest Hillis daughter. As March drew to a close, it seemed clear that this was not to be. Everyone knew that Margaret would not be with the family for three more weeks.

But the God who had provided milk for her babies and protected her husband in China years earlier had one more miracle for Margaret. On April 1, Michelle Renee Hawthorne was born in Portland, Oregon—three weeks before she was expected. And less than a week later she was placed in her grandmother's arms. Too weak to close her arms tightly around the baby, Margaret was strong enough to pray a sweet prayer of blessing for her tiny granddaughter.

Days later, as Nancy sat at her mother's bedside, Margaret insisted on discussing with her the subject of Dick's remarriage.

"I've made a list of who I think would make a good wife for Dick," she confided in her daughter.

"Mother, for his own survival I agree it may be best for him to remarry," Nancy answered. "But I absolutely refuse to talk names with you. Please, if there really is a list, destroy it! If Dad ever found it he'd rush out and marry the 'top' person on it just to please you."

Pleasing Margaret was Dick's only concern. His life revolved around trying to make her as comfortable as possible, tempting her to eat a little, listening for her in the night.

Two weeks before her death, Dick lay on a cot beside her bed listening for her, praying for her. In the quiet, dark hours, the still, small voice of the Spirit whispered to him, "I'm taking My child home."

"You have the right to take the fruit when it is ripe, Father," Dick responded. "She is ripe."

A few days later, Muriel Cook visited Margaret. "Pray with me," Margaret pleaded, "that God will give Dick someone to help him finish the race."

She was peaceful as they prayed that God would provide someone to run with Dick the last lap.

Family members came to stay in April and to help Dick with Margaret's care. Margaret's brother and sister-in-law, Louis and Helen Humphrey, and her sister, Virginia Davis, brought new energy and encouragement into the house as they helped Dick in the kitchen and took turns sitting with Margaret, giving Dick brief respites from the long hours of her care. Brian and his wife, Susie, arrived bringing with them additional support and help.

Because Susie and Helen were both registered nurses, Margaret was able to stay at home and receive expert medical care.

During those days Margaret talked much about going "home." Once when her appetite ebbed, Dick encouraged her to eat. But she responded,

"Dear, how long do I have to continue eating this 'earth food'?"

"Honey, this could be your last meal down here, I don't know," Dick answered. "But the Good Shepherd has His timing, His clock, His calendar, and He will tell you when you have to eat the last one."

"Earth clothes" and "earth days" were often referred to in her conversation. On April 10, she said, "Oh, I thought I would have left my 'earth clothes' behind and been in heaven now, at home."

Five days later, on April 15, 1981, she did "change clothes." She stepped into a new robe, the one described by the prophet Isaiah as the "garments of salvation, the robe of righteousness," put on with a shout of joy!

At a memorial service, Norm Cook, the Hillises' long-time intimate friend, said, "As I think about Margaret and think about missions, I think of cultures and the changing of cultures. When you go to another country you always go through culture shock because there are always so many changes. Of all the people I know, Margaret Hillis would have the least culture shock in heaven because she lived it so much here on earth."

The wise king of the Proverbs says of the virtuous woman, "Her children arise up and call her blessed." And so they did. "Many daughters have done virtuously, but thou excellest them all. . . . Give her the fruit of her hands; and let her own works praise her in the gates" (Proverbs 31:28-29, 31).

26

Second Wind

Dick Hillis was known to be zealous—a man in a hurry. But then a man who is zealous for the salvation of entire nations, anxious to see world evangelism accomplished during his lifetime, would be characterized as a man in a hurry.

Margaret's home-going did not suddenly change that, and neither did it alter the focus of his goal. It simply increased his desire to finish the race and reach "home."

Dick was determined to finish the race he had begun nearly fifty years earlier in such a way as to bring glory to the One who had chosen him for the race. He constantly repeated to himself the words the Apostle Paul wrote to Timothy about his race, "I have fought a good fight, I have finished the course, I have kept the faith." "Dear Lord," he prayed, "I want to be able to say that. Help me, Lord, to keep running a straight course."

The place in the Father's house the Lord Jesus said He was preparing had always been important to Dick and Margaret. Her "home-going" only increased the importance of heaven to Dick. He tried to imagine what it would be like to be beholding the Savior's face and to be with those he loved forever. The thought that multiplied millions of people knew nothing of heaven drove Dick as never before. In the ten months following Margaret's death, Dick carried the message of life over 62,000 miles. The heavy schedule he admitted was hard on him physically, but it was therapeutic to his spirit.

When Dick arrived in Manila, his son, Steve, an OC missionary, could not help but notice his thin, exhausted state when he met him at the airport. He was alarmed at his father's loss of weight and his obvious fatigue.

"What are you trying to do to yourself, Dad?" Steve exclaimed. His voice and his expression carried the concern he felt for his father as he looked at Dick's haggard appearance. "Are you trying to kill yourself?"

"Not really," Dick replied, "but I guess I am in a hurry to break the tape that says the race is over. Don't worry about me. Hard work is good for me. Believe me, Steve, I am much more fulfilled in serving than I would be sitting in that little house in California. Those four walls hold no joy for me since your mom went home. You know, I will soon be three score and ten years, so I don't have much longer to run."

"Wait a minute, Dad," Steve replied. "I don't accept your reasoning. Aren't you in danger of playing God? Who told you that you only had another year? God may have another ten or even twenty years in His plan for you."

Steve's words shocked Dick like voltage from a hot wire. God had centuries ago spoken to Israel through Jeremiah, "For I know the plans that I have for you . . . plans of welfare and not for calamity to give you a future and a hope" (Jeremiah 29:11, NASB). Was the same loving God trying to get Dick's attention? Was his plan for Dick a second wind—a future and a hope?

"Steve, I know you will understand when I confess that it is hard to run alone. I don't think I could run for another ten years. I am afraid I would fail." Dick finally expressed the fear that had haunted him in the months since Margaret's death had left him a widower.

"I do understand, Dad, but is it possible that God has prepared someone to continue the race with you?"

It was a long flight home from Manila to San Francisco. Dick was tired, but his mind was wide awake. Did God want him to marry again? Was a loving Father preparing someone to run with him?

"Thy will be done on earth in my life, Father, as the angels do it in heaven," Dick prayed. Before the big plane let down at the airport in San Francisco Dick knew the Lord would reveal His will. He had many times assured others seeking to know God's will with the exhortation to remember "God will never hide His will for any child who will do His will." Now he applied it to himself.

He recalled a verse, Psalm 32:8: "I will instruct thee and teach thee in the way which thou shalt go: I will guide thee with mine eye." He suddenly had a special sense of the Father's eye upon him. It had long been a comfort to him that God's eye is constantly upon His children.

The verse gave him the courage to take a long, hard look at the race set

before him, to realign his view of the track with that of the Father's.
He began to pray earnestly about a mate to run with him the last lap of the
"earth race."

During hours of thoughtful prayer only one name came to mind, and that
was Ruth Kopperud's.

Dick had known Ruth for eighteen years. She worked in the OC offices.
He saw her quiet, beautiful spirit, her prayer life, and her love for Jesus
Christ. He wondered if she was the one he needed to help him continue and
finish the race. He prayed until he felt confident that God was leading him,
then he went to see her.

Ruth had been intent on listening to what God had to say to her since
meeting Jesus Christ as a young woman of twenty-one. Her plan was to go to
Japan as a missionary following graduation from Simpson Bible College.
But World War II interrupted those plans. Ruth wasted no time in finding
God's next directives. She attended Missionary Medical School, business
school, and went to work with the Canadian Sunday School Mission. Later
she served in a mission hospital for the Bella Bella Indians in British
Columbia.

In January 1964, she joined the headquarters staff at Overseas Crusades.
During her years as part of the mission she became a well-loved friend of the
Hillis family.

Dick expressed in a letter that "it was no coincidence that Ruth was one of
the last family friends to gather with us around Margaret's bed and pray for
her before her home-going."

Sunday, Valentine's Day 1982, Dick decided to go and speak to Ruth about
what was going on in his heart. He asked her for an hour of her time. In Hillis
fashion, direct and determined, he told her of his great admiration for her.

"In no way do I want our friendship harmed," he said. "If what is going on
in my heart is not going on in yours, I will understand. Ruth, I will stop right
now if that is your wish."

"Dick, please don't stop!" Ruth answered. "Let me tell you what is going
on in my heart. For weeks I have sensed growing preoccupation for you in
my heart. I too, have been praying."

Dick and Ruth looked at the Scriptures that God had used to reassure Ruth
that His hand was directing the events of her life as well as her love for Dick.

"Last week I prayed, 'Please, Lord, either take him out of my thoughts or
bring him to me!' "

Seven weeks later, in April, God brought them together in marriage.

Dick wrote to his family and friends, "She is God's gift to help me on the
last 'earth mile.'

"We are so aware that God planned it and planted in our hearts this love for one another. Back in eternity past this was ordained by God—doubt is totally impossible. How good the Lord is!

"I feel I have a second wind to finish the race. We will run it together."

Once before Dick had felt that second wind. Thirty-two years earlier he had stood on the bow of the *General Gordon* and experienced the breath of God blowing assurance of a continuing ministry. Though his life in mainland China had ended, his life as a missionary had not. His exit from China had meant his entrance into the whole world. God had given him a new life when he thought his life was over.

It seemed God was again renewing his servant. Dick's revived interest in life brought a renewal of vision. More ambitious than ever was the world Christian who was now impatient with the too-short hours of each day. His prayer now was that he would be blessed with enough years of life to see his vision fulfilled—that he would live to see the whole world evangelized.

Dr. Donald McGavran, long time friend of Overseas Crusades, missionary statesman, theologian, and scholar, once said, "It is not June, it is September. It is not planting time, it is harvest time."

A sense of urgency overwhelmed Dick. And it seemed to permeate the entire mission as well. So much of the world was ripe for harvest. Reports poured in from around the globe telling of the vast numbers of believers being revived and mobilized to reach their own nations.

Plans were formulated for the articulation of one of the major distinctives of the mission—that of full-nation focus. The dream of seeing an entire nation evangelized seemed a possibility in the near future. Guatemala was to be the sight of the first Discipling A Whole Nation (DAWN) Congress. Not since the early days of ministry in Taiwan had the mission known such excitement.

A similar effort had been made in the Philippines in 1971, and its success was still a source of encouragement and motivation to the mission. "Christ the Only Way" (COW) Movement had seen thousands of Filipinos make decisions for Jesus Christ.

Anticipation was high as the mission prayed and considered its forward movement into the world. But Dick was troubled.

How can we believe that we are reaching into the uttermost parts of the earth while China, containing one-fourth of the world's population, is not being taught or discipled? he asked himself.

It had been fifty years since he had accepted the task of ministering to China's people. Though he had fled the country seventeen years later, he had never been able to escape the burden of China's unevangelized millions.

Through his many years of missionary service he had become a world Christian, but deep within his soul there would always be a singular devotion to the people of China.

His second wind seemed to be stirring up feelings of discontent within him. He would not be satisfied until, once again, Jesus, the Bread of Life, could be offered to the hungry millions in his adopted homeland, China.

27

Return to China

The main street of Shanghai was alive with morning activity—people moving in every direction, shouting, bickering, laughing. Bicycle wheels rolled along the road, and children ran in and out of doorways. On the Bund [German name given to the waterfront], people gathered to begin their ritualistic calisthenics. Groups of twenty, forty, and more, most of them elderly, moved together in slow rhythm, stretching, leaning, pulling muscles into position, then releasing to stretch and pull again.

From the Hope Hotel window, Dick Hillis watched the scene. The hotel had been called the Park when he stayed in it nearly half a century ago. But it was now October 1982, and with the years had come change. Dick glanced behind him at the old room and once again regretted the nostalgic urge that had prompted him to stay here. The paint on the walls was peeling off, the faucets appeared to have dripped for the past fifty years, and the rusted porcelain fixtures no longer functioned.

Dick's eyes left the hotel room to roam across the city. The rest of Shanghai seemed untouched by the passing of years. There were no new buildings in sight, no signs of new construction or progress. It was as if time had refused to leave a mark on the port city that had charmed the world for centuries.

The streets are a little cleaner than I remember them, he thought. Then his eyes returned to the view of the harbor. *That hasn't changed,* Dick thought with a smile, as he gazed at the huge ships and the small boats that bobbed around them like excited children at a mother's skirt.

Shanghai was much the same as it had always been. But the passing of forty-nine years had changed Dick Hillis. In October 1933 he had been an idealistic youth, an impatient third-class passenger on a "slow boat to China." He had come believing he could do something for China. He had been frightened, appalled, offended, and revolted—all in the first few moments after his feet had left the gangplank and touched the cobblestones of Shanghai's streets.

Dick could smile now at the memory of the range of emotions he had experienced that first day in Shanghai, though at the time he had felt more like crying than smiling. He continued to smile as he thought of his recent pleasant journey to the port city via jet flight, with his bride, Ruth, accompanying him. He turned to look at her and breathed a prayer of thanks for her presence with him on this trip. It was a trip into his past, and, he prayed, a trip into the possibilities for the future.

The goal for the journey was to discover what they could about the church in China and to determine how they, as a mission could best serve God while serving the church in China.

Dick had only recently allowed himself to hope that he could revisit China someday. Since she had begun to ease relations with the western world a few years earlier, China had allowed tour groups to enter the country and had begun to encourage cultural exchange. After months of planning, the mission organized a tour group and asked Chuck Holsinger, veteran missionary and vice-president, to lead it.

Already they had spent time in Canton, Peking, Nanking, and Suchow. The government prohibited them from visiting the remote inland regions where Dick had begun his missionary work, and though he was disappointed, he satisfied himself by reminding himself that he was at least in China again.

Sunday in Shanghai found Dick and Ruth and the rest of the tour seated in the balcony of the Moore Tabernacle, the largest church in Shanghai. Thirty-two years earlier, only weeks before the Communists had forced him out of the country, Dick and Dave Morken had led a seven-day youth conference in that church. His mind kept straying back to the memories, and he had to force himself to concentrate on the service that was going on around him.

He admired the robed choir and noticed that they all had hymnals and Bibles. The majority of the congregation, however, had none. He listened to the preacher and was pleased to hear him preaching from the Bible. But he knew, though the pastor had been trained by a missionary thirty years earlier, he was now employed by the government. He was among the last of the existing missionary-trained pastors. The next generation of pastors would have little or no understanding of biblical truth and its application to practical living, for the Bible schools and seminaries had been closed for over three decades. Missionaries had been gone from the land for as long.

Only government-approved churches were allowed to meet. These were registered with the state and pastored by state-approved, registered pastors. The practice of religion was allowed, only as it agreed with the philosophy of religion as stated by the Peking system.

A great wave of depression swept over Dick as he sat there, listening, thinking of the thousands of believers forced to meet secretly in "house churches" because they refused to agree with the government's philosophy of religion. Their leaders faced imprisonment, torture, and prison camp if discovered.

But there was also cause for rejoicing, Dick reminded himself. Though there had been no missionary in China for more than three decades, the church had grown. Though there were no more than a million evangelical believers in China in 1950, it was believed that number had now grown to between 25 and 50 million. The imprisonment and persecution had not stifled the church of Jesus Christ but rather, as in Paul the apostle's day, had brought about the "greatest progress of the gospel" (Philippians 1:12-14).

Yet difficulties faced the valiant church. Bibles were forbidden, Sunday school meetings prohibited. All seminaries and Bible schools had been closed. The result was a dearth in leadership. The fast-growing church was crowded with millions of "new babies" who, without the clear teaching of the Bible, would be open targets for deception and confusion in their newfound faith.

Dick's heart echoed again Hudson Taylor's cry "Poor neglected China!"

Again he asked himself, "How can we as a mission say we are fulfilling the Great Commission if we are ignoring the needs of the country that contains a fourth of the world's population?"

But an even more persistent question plagued him as he looked over the huge congregation that had gathered in the tabernacle that Sunday. *How* can they be helped? Spiritual malnutrition threatens them, but how can they be fed?

He knew the government would never allow missionaries to come into the country again. Though the Peking statement boasted of a measure of "religious freedom," it was freedom as defined by the state. Those who practiced religion of a form approved by the state would be allowed to practice it freely.

Conventional missionary methods could never again be used in China, yet Dick was convinced that the great need of China's church was the daily teaching of the Word of God.

Suddenly it was clear to Dick. There *was* a way to teach and disciple this huge nation. Radio! He looked out over the congregation and he knew, with an assurance that only the Holy Spirit can give, that radio was the answer to China's great need for the daily teaching of the Word of God.

Excitement began to build in him as he thought about the possibilities. All Chinese citizens were urged to have radios in order to listen to propaganda broadcasts aired daily by the state-operated radio stations. What was to prevent those same radios from receiving the life-giving messages of Jesus Christ?

Radio broadcasts could do in China what missionaries could never do. God's Word could ride the air waves into every Chinese home. The nation could be taught and discipled by radio.

Dick's mind was busy with ideas and questions. He could hardly wait for the service to be over so he could relate his thoughts to the others of his group. Already he was certain: radio was the means of feeding the hungry in China. Already a plan was forming.

Thirty-three years earlier, a man named Robert Bowman had had a vision of reaching China by radio broadcasts. President Chiang, before his final overthrow on the mainland, had offered him a piece of property in Nanking to build a radio station and begin the work. Bobby Bowman decided however, to make his base of operation Manila. There he had established what became known as Radio City and the Far East Broadcasting Company, or FEBC. He asked Dick to join him and take charge of the Mandarin messages. Dick could no longer minister in the inland provinces and was at that time considering what God was leading him to do next. He put the decision to his directors in the China Inland Mission. The mission's leadership felt the work was not consistent with their inland-based philosophy of ministry. So Dick turned down the invitation.

In the ensuing years FEBC grew and placed transmitters in several Asian nations. If Overseas Crusades could use their transmitters, pay for the radio time, Dick thought, and prepare Bible study materials, they could preach to China, disciple the believers there, and train the laity.

Dick returned home to America with one consuming thought: to do whatever was necessary to begin broadcasting into China as soon as possible. Several months of preparation lay ahead. Christian workers in Hong Kong prepared Bible study materials. Dick traveled and presented the need of China's church to believers across the country. The mission budget had not anticipated this new ministry, so additional funds had to be sought to help pay for the upkeep of the powerful transmitters and for the helpers in Hong Kong.

"Prayer is our greatest need," Dick declared to Christian congregations across the country. "Pray that the Word of God will penetrate the bamboo curtain and the church will be discipled and mobilized to evangelize the whole nation of China. It *can* be done," he said with confidence. "The believers in China have grown from one million to perhaps as many as fifty million. This they have done with little or no leadership, with few Bibles, and with no help from the rest of the Christian world, aside from the faithful prayers of those who have cared enough to pray for them in the years since China has been closed.

"We want to give them Bibles, disciple them, and help bring them to maturity in Christ through daily Bible study classes. This fast-growing church must be fed for Jesus Christ."

On May 1, 1983, Overseas Crusades began broadcasting a six-day-a-week church leadership Bible School of the Air. From Cheju Island in Korea, FEBC's 250,000-watt transmitter hurled the daily lesson into China. From the eastern coast of China to the Tibetan border, in both long and short wave, the radio message the Voice of Friendship could be heard.

A few weeks after broadcasting began, the responses from Christians and non-Christians in every province of China started arriving in the FEBC office in Hong Kong.

A listener in Anhui wrote, "We are indeed the weakest ones in the body of Christ. We desperately need your prayers."

Christians in Henan wrote to say, "There are almost 90 percent of the contents in your programs which we have never heard before. It is so precious to us."

A desperate plea came from a teenager in Guangxi:

> I am quite despair as I look into the future. I would rather die than drag on with a hopeless life, but committing suicide cannot be a way out. Just at this moment of confusion and frustration, I have thought of writing to you for your kind advice and encouragement. I need your help desperately, and I will be most thankful for your guidance rendered to me.

The letters received in the FEBC office were forwarded to Dick at the Overseas Crusades headquarters. He read them through a blur of tears, recognizing in them the polite, sincere spirit that had charmed and humbled him for half a century.

Requests for Bibles and other Christian literature as well as song books came in many of the letters. A believer from Henan wrote:

> I was overjoyed with tears as I received the precious Bible from you. The Word of God is what I need to grow and be matured in faith. I am a faithful listener.

. . . My beloved little girl died before I received the Bibles. I was in deep sorrow and was weak in faith. My wife was more depressed even than I was. Thanks to God that the Bible came to hand just in time to save us from our weakness. The Word of God has revived our faith. Brothers and sisters are encouraged. . . . Many of us have little education and we don't usually have a pastor around to guide us. Now all these programs have provided for the guidance we need.

In every letter Dick read the affirmation of God's leading in the radio ministry into China. One letter outlined in poignant detail the circumstances his Chinese brothers faced daily in the province of Anhui.

Recently I have heard the Discipleship training program which you spoke about the church, evangelism, etc. I am very much interested in what you say. I trust this program will be a beneficial to the house churches here.

I accepted the Lord for almost two years. During these past months the situation here are quite unstable. The preachers has already gone, and the churches scattered and located in different areas, and we have no preachers in our midst, so they asked me to read the Bible and speak. With much hesitation I said, 'I have no message!' Therefore they pray for me earnestly before the Lord and now we are learning together in the Word of God. After a while when the situation is turning better, then we can gather together again. However, at the moment, we scattered again.

Questions about salvation, baptism, and Bible doctrines filled the letters. Non-Christians and Christians alike were hearing for the first time such terms as *trinity* and *salvation,* and they wondered at the meanings of such words.

In one letter came the question, What happens to a pastor who can't endure the suffering and pressure and finally deviates from the Lord and the truth? It was a stark reminder of the persecution that threatened the Christian leaders in China.

Writing letters of response consumed hundreds of hours from the broadcasting team and their staff. Requests for reading materials and Bibles were processed as quickly as possible. Other letters questioned why the Bibles and books had not yet been received. No doubt they had been held up by postal customs.

"I don't know what happen to the mail . . . but I haven't got any response yet. I am very discourage . . . however, no matter what, I still trust you. Please write me as soon as possible."

Though patient and polite in their queries, China's people were hungry, starving for the Bread of Life. For so long they had subsisted on the most meager portions of spiritual food. Now their appetite had been whetted and they could not be content with only small, limited servings offered at scheduled broadcast times.

Dick carefully read the letters on his desk. He was thankful that OC had now joined FEBC and others in helping to feed the spiritual hunger of the believers in China. Christians were being taught and discipled; the lost evangelized. Radio had penetrated the bamboo curtain that for three decades had muffled the happy news. The sound barrier had been broken.

For centuries China had been a country characterized by walls: walls built to keep out aggressors, walls erected to prevent the influence of outsiders. The Great Wall, though once effective in keeping out the unwanted, ultimately fell victim to the advances of civilization. The founders of the Peking government attempted to isolate their people from the power and influence of the "Nothing-He-Cannot-Do-One," and for three decades they thought they had succeeded.

But Jesus said, "I will build My church; and the gates of Hades shall not overpower it" (Matthew 16:18, NASB). Nor shall brick walls, bamboo curtains, or isolationist philosophies of government.

Perhaps the Christians in China understand better than any the meaning of Paul's words "neither death, nor life, nor angels, nor principalities, nor things present, nor things to come, nor powers, nor height, nor depth, nor any other created thing, shall be able to separate us from the love of God which is in Christ Jesus our Lord" (Romans 8:38-39, NASB).

A young boy's dream of China had come full circle. The childhood fantasy of treasure and wealth beyond compare became reality for Dick Hillis when he discovered the riches of grace in Christ Jesus. His consuming interest in life became service to his Lord.

Once asked what he believed would be an appropriate logo for Overseas Crusades, Dick answered, "A towel. Jesus picked up a towel and washed the feet of His disciples. He came to serve and to minister. We must do as He did, be servants to the whole body of Christ. And our badge, our symbol, is that of a towel."

Oswald Chambers wrote, "To serve God is the deliberate love-gift of a nature that has heard the call of God."

Since he first heard the call of God, Dick Hillis's life has been a deliberate love-gift. He understood, above all things, that the servant is not greater than the master.

Bibliography

Chai, Ch'u, and Chai, Winberg. *The Changing Society of China*. New York: New American Library, 1962.

Chambers, Oswald. *My Utmost for His Highest*. New York: Dodd, Mead, 1935.

Hillis, Dick. *China Assignment*. Palo Alto, Calif.: Overseas Crusades, n.d.

————. *Unlock the Heavens*. Henderson, Neb.: Service, n.d.

Pollock, J. C. *Hudson Taylor and Maria*. Grand Rapids: Zondervan, 1967.

Tozer, A.W. *The Pursuit of God*. Special ed. Wheaton: Tyndale, n.d.

Wilson, Kenneth L. *Angel At Her Shoulder*. New York: Harper & Row, 1964.